New Horizons
for the Priesthood

New Horizons
for the Priesthood

by Andrew M. Greeley

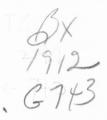

SHEED & WARD   NEW YORK

Manufactured in the United States of America

For Ernest J. Primeau
Bishop of Manchester
(not the British one)

— Teacher and Friend

Contents

New Horizons
for the Priesthood

Introduction

Since he's the one who discovered it, Erik Erikson probably has some right to say what the proper use of the term "identity crisis" ought to be. In his recent book, *Identity and the Life Cycle*,* Erikson expresses surprise that the phrase he almost took for granted had become a staple of popular psychology. One has the impression that he is generally pleased with the popularity of his brain child, but that there are also some reservations:

> I must register a certain impatience with the equation never suggested by me of the term "identity" with the question, "Who am I?" This question nobody would ask himself, except in a more or less transient, morbid state . . . wherefore, on occasion, I find myself asking a student who claims that he is in an "identity crisis" whether he's complaining or boasting. The pertinent question, if it can be put in the first person at all, would be, "What do I want to make of myself?" and "What do I have to work with?"

* New York: International Univs. Press, 1967.

Anyone who has dealt with young people in extensive counseling relationships knows that the question "Who am I?" is all too frequently a self-pitying and self-deceiving question. It is a demand for sympathy, for special treatment and for the right to withdraw from one's ordinary obligations and commitments. It is an "identity crisis" aimed at stagnation and immobility, and, while it provides ample occasion for serious conversation, it is also a permanent excuse from activity and growth.

It often seems to me that much of the discussion about "priestly identity" or about the "identity crisis of the priesthood" is of the variety which Erikson is not willing to permit to be called "identity crisis." When a priest, young or old, says "I don't know what the priest is," he frequently seems to me to be in the more or less "transient, morbid state" which, in itself, has nothing to do with identity. I am also afraid that the morbidity is likely to be less transient rather than more transient.

If, therefore, we are to take Erikson's whole psychology seriously and not merely use one of his terms carelessly, the important questions to be asked in an authentic identity crisis of the priesthood are: what do we want to make of the priesthood, and what do we have to work with? The questions then are dynamic ones. They ask not so much what the priesthood is now, but where it came from, and in what direction we intend to move it. There is no room for self-pity in such a question, no room for withdrawal of commitments, no room for a refusal to grow or to move. Erikson's identity crisis, like that of Cardinal Suhard, is a crisis of growth and not of decline, much less of immobility.

The same idea was expressed in different categories by the Reverend John Shea:

> For in each age the Christian priest has tried to make the mark of Christ on his own culture—according to his notion of priest and his notion of culture. And something of the priesthood of each age always survives to spill over into the next and so establish continuity between the priesthood of yesterday and the priesthood of today. But, there is no reason to dote on this continuity. It is present and that is enough. The task is discontinuity, growth, fidelity to the future. The task is to find the cultural form of priesthood that will present the most possibilities for the meaning of Jesus to penetrate our civilization. Fidelity is not sameness, and by some paradox faithfulness to the future, which necessarily involves change, is also faithfulness to the past. Discontinuity is continuity, for only by being discontinuous with the cultural form of priesthood can we be continuous with the meaning of priesthood. We must always seek the greatest possible making-present of God in the world.

The identity of the priesthood then is a crisis of growth, a crisis of simultaneity of continuity and discontinuity, the crisis of creating the future, the crisis of "the greatest possible making-present of God in the world." One does not blot out the past and wander aimlessly in a circle wondering what one ought to do. One rather sees a vision of the future and makes an act of commitment to the creation of the reality of this vision. It is time that American priests put behind them the luxury of self-pity and become what they ought to be, creators of the future.

A classic example of this self-pity was in the title (though not in the content) of Father Joseph Fichter's recent book, *America's Forgotten Priests: What Are They Saying?** The irony of the title was underscored by the fact that it appeared the same week that *Look* published the most recent installment of "The Life and Loves of America's Favorite Former Priest." Far from being forgotten, the priest has never received so much publicity. Indeed, the last year might well be called "The Year of the Priest" since the newspapers were filled with accounts of former priests, priests about to leave, priests who wanted to get married, priests who had gotten married, priests who had lost their faith, priests who defied their bishops, and priests who have organized against their bishops. If the priesthood is going out of style, it's going out of style not with a whimper, but with a bang.

The priests who catch the headlines, who appear on the "Johnny Carson Show," or announce to assembled multitudes at Notre Dame University that they are going to marry are not, of course, typical priests, though their problems may represent in exaggerated fashion many of the fears and the anxieties that have disturbed a substantial number of priests. The critical problem, however, is not that the priesthood is in crisis. The issue is where we go from the crisis. And the crisis is a serious one, surely the worst since the French Revolution, and possibly the worst since the Reformation. But it is a peculiar kind of crisis, a crisis generated in substantial part by the fact that the social structure of the Church is not changing as rapidly as

* New York: Harper & Row, 1965.

people's ideas and enthusiasm. It is not that the Church lacks vitality, but rather that there is too much vitality for the present outmoded structures.

Something is dying in the Church. The image of the priest which served most of us until the early 1960's is dying in the laity and is dying in us, too. The parish priest went to wakes, funerals and wedding receptions, visited the sick in the hospitals and was always in the rectory waiting for the sick call when it came. He spent his days off and vacations with other priests and was afraid to become too closely involved with the laity for fear it would be a threat to his vocation. He is rapidly becoming extinct, and the new priest, the creator of the future, is replacing him. I'm not trying to argue that the priest is the only one that creates the future. The scientist does, too. So does the poet, the metaphysician and the prophet; but the priest is one of the critical creators of the future because, as in Father Shea's words, his task is the "making-present of God in the world." We will leave aside in the present volume the rather foolish question of how the priest's "making-present of God" differs from the layman's. It seems to me that as long as the question is discussed in these terms, it will never be solved. It suffices to say that the priest deals with the ultimate vision of where mans' pilgrimage is going—the ultimate that is not only at the end of the pilgrimage, but is also dynamically present in our midst. The priest creates the future because he believes in the future and transmits this faith to his people.

This book points towards the future which the priest must help to create since our dream of the future is still inchoate. The present volume will deal more with the virtues to be required of the creator of the future than with a precise explication of what that future will be like. The virtues are those that are required of men living and working in a dramatic transition, men struggling simultaneously with continuity and discontinuity. Our descriptions of the specific virtues will emphasize both the continuity and the discontinuity, those things out of the past which must be salvaged and those things which must be created anew in our strain towards the future. It may seem that we push only a little way out of the past into the future; but the new priesthood is so very new, and our understanding of it is so very imperfect that "a little way" is all the progress we can make at the present time. But even a little progress gets us off the dead center on which we currently seem to be stuck. It forces us to ask not *who we are,* but the much more relevant question, *where are we going?* The pace of the pilgrimage has speeded up so fast that it makes us dizzy. So virtues of priests must be virtues not merely of men on a pilgrimage, but of the advance guides, the scouts, who are at the head of the pilgrimage going into the wilderness, exploring the unknown and leading the way into the future.

Erikson says, as I mentioned earlier, that he asked a young man who reports his identity crisis whether he is boasting or complaining. It is clear in Erikson's own view that identity crisis is something about which to boast because it is not so much a reassessment of what one is, but of what one hopes to accomplish. Such a reassessment is something to be proud of. Headlines are currently being seized by those clergy whose reassessment has led them to give up and to decide for one reason or another that as priests they are not going anywhere. Without making any judgment at all on these men, we can still say that most priests will not make this decision. Some, indeed the best, will determine where they are going and then begin to move in that direction. Those who leave will shortly be forgotten as are so many other of the "personalities" that appear all too briefly in the pages of the popular journals and on the television screen. Those who have the courage to face the question of where we are going and provide some kind of tentative answer will not be forgotten. If their individual names are forgotten, their work will live forever. It is for this kind of priest that the present volume is written for discussion of the qualities necessary for men who are willing to be the trailblazers in the pilgrimage to the Absolute.

Some things must be said about the context within which we are to create the future. There has emerged in recent years a vast literature on the future from science fiction utopias to the very serious work of men like Daniel Bell, Herman Kahn, Fritz Baade and Robert Heilbroner, whose books are often more startling than the wildest of science fiction.

In another volume,* I have described in some considerable detail my own feelings about the possibilities and the hazards of the next half century. It is technically possible for us to eliminate most material poverty in the world. We are making rapid progress in understanding the sources and roots of distrust, suspicion and hatred. We are, I think, on the verge of a breakthrough in human love,

---

* *Religion in the Year 2000* (New York: Sheed & Ward, 1969).

particularly in that primal relationship of love between man and woman. We are in the process of forming new friendship communities where there is more trust and social support than men have ever been able to offer to their fellowmen in the past. It is conceivable that we might reorganize society on the basis of such friendship communities and that our rapid progress in transportation and communication would extend friendship throughout the whole world. Since we no longer need fear the material world, we are, for the first time, in the position to convert it into a playground and a park which man can simultaneously enjoy and respect.

At the same time, the potentialities for destruction are immense. Ethnic hatred now has at its service far more sophisticated weapons than in the past; the population explosion is as serious a menace as it ever was; giant corporate bodies have threatened to depersonalize and dehumanize life in the affluent society; and the human race is on the verge of certain irrevocable decisions. These decisions will lead to a great evolutionary leap forward or to a regression into a barbarianism that will be none the less barbaric for the fact that it may be technologically affluent and organizationally sophisticated. The options are running out. Human society will either be transformed, or it will be caught in disaster, a disaster of destruction or giantism.

One can, in such circumstances, be either an optimist or a pessimist, depending largely, I suspect, on one's own personality style. One can be optimistic or pessimistic if one is not a Christian. For a Christian neither alternative is feasible because the Christian must be a man of hope.

He believes in the Resurrection; he believes in the Risen Saviour among us; he believes in the promise of the Resurrection to come and of the process of Resurrection going on now. Man and man's world are destined for Resurrection, and, therefore, mankind will survive. More than that, the vision of faith says that mankind will survive in and through the Church because the Church is the Resurrection promise alive among us. The poor, battered, messed-up Roman Catholic Church is still mankind's best hope because mankind's hope is to be found most completely in the Church.

Man's destiny at this present point in history depends on man's relationships. If we grow in trust, friendship and love, then mankind will survive. If we do not grow in trust and in love, mankind will return to barbarianism. Our faith must be that the Church will lead mankind by showing, in virtue of the Resurrection promise within it, the quality of relationships possible among human beings. "By this will all men know that you are my disciples, if you have love for one another" (John 13:35) and "See how these Christians love one another." (Tertullian). The Church then creates the future by leading the way, by demonstrating the splendor and the possibility of human love. Given the nature of the present crisis, the Church will probably create the future whether it wants to or not.

The priest is the relational man par excellence in the Church. He's the man whose love must show within the Church the meaning and the possibility of love. The priest is involved in the making-present of God in the world precisely through the quality of his relationships. The new priesthood which is emerging will eventually lead the

Church and mankind through its present crisis to the greatest evolutionary leap forward since we came out of the trees. For the man of faith, this new priesthood is being formed by the Lord whether we like it or not. The present question of identity is really a question of how long it will take us to recognize that this is our mission as priests. It is a question of how long we will resist the winds of the Holy Spirit before we discover the direction in which they are blowing.

[1]

Hope

I have, perhaps, a perspective on the Church and on the priesthood that few others have been able to enjoy. Half of my life as a priest was spent very much within the institutional pre-Vatican Church, although I must say in retrospect that in most ways the parish in which I served represented the best of traditional Catholicism. But the second half of my life as a priest has been spent very much on the margins of the institutional Church. My work at a research center at a secular university, my salary, my insurance, my retirement benefits are paid for by the Center. My research interests have moved from the sociology of religion to the sociology of ethnic groups, and from the study of Catholic education and Catholic higher education to more general problems of personality development in higher education. My colleagues are, for the most part, non-Catholics and agnostics. My work is generally respected by my secular colleagues, though not particularly valued by my fellow priests or by my archdiocese, and questioned by the Catholic press. Though I do have a pastoral involvement of my own, I have very little connection with the traditional parish and the traditional arch-diocese, and I spend little time doing those kinds of things which were once defined as the essence of priestly work. I am far more involved in the secular world than are most priests, and I am, indeed, more secular than most of the professional Catholic laymen who are currently preaching the gospel of secularity.

I would have thought when I was a seminarian and a younger priest that such an existence on the margins of the ecclesiastical institution would be dangerous and that my priesthood and my faith would be threatened. But I have learned to my surpise that both my vocation and my faith are much stronger and much safer here on the margins than they were in the center of the institutional activity. The ties that bind me to the institutional Church are few. For example, I could easily earn my living without being a priest. Paradoxically, the ties are very strong, and I cannot conceive of any situation in which I would not be a priest. Curiously enough, some of my friends have labeled my activity "hyphenated priesthood." Very definitely they are using the word "hyphenated" in the pejorative sense. I am at a loss to understand this criticism, for the ones who make it are the same ones who are eager to ordain pro-fessional men as priests. Apparently they cannot accept the idea of a priest being a professional sociologist. Similarly, they were in the past quite enthusiastic about the idea of priests workers. Now they seem unable to accept that work when it is done at the National Opinion Research Center. But more of this subject in a later chapter.

This somewhat lengthy personal introduction is a pre-lude to saying that from my position out here on the margin of the American Church, I find myself growing ever more hopeful about the future of American Catholicism. Not only do I feel more of a priest and more of a churchman on the boundary line between the Church and the secular world, but I am, heaven save me, a more optimistic churchman.

I've often wondered what the reason for this phenomenon is. In part, I suppose I'm impressed by the fascination and eager enthusiasm of my secular colleagues about the change in Roman Catholicism. In part, I can afford to be hopeful because I am spared the hundred and one annoyances that many of those who are still working in the more traditional church must experience every day. In part, it is because as a sociologist I have a somewhat more sophisticated understanding of the nature of social change than do many of my colleagues in the institutional Church, and I can appreciate somewhat better the meaning of the change that is taking place. But the basic reason, I think, and it is a reason that sums up all the others, is that I have been fortunate enough, in God's providence, to be in a position where I can see not only the trees, but the forest, and a healthy, vigorous and promising forest it is.

From my perspective it is very difficult for me to see why someone would want to leave. I understand, of course, that there are casualties in any transition, and I certainly do not wish to make judgments about anyone. To leave the priesthood is to withdraw commitment, but sometimes withdrawal of an ill-advised commitment is an essential step to maturity. I understand that some men have been virtually driven from the priesthood, and I deeply sympathize with their suffering. I have somewhat less sympathy with those whose need to justify their own action leads them to attack the church and to try to persuade others to leave.

Having said all these things, I still find it difficult to really understand why people leave. To leave the priesthood seems to mean that one has given up hope in the priesthood. Try as I may, I can interpret this in no other way than as a tragic misreading of the data. It seems to me, and I say this with some very clear rememberance of the frustrations of being an assistant pastor in a traditional parish, that there has never been a time in the history of the priesthood when it has been more exciting or more challenging to be a priest.

In my own rather peculiar position on the margins, I've come in contact with a number of former priests, and I must report that in general they do not seem to be a very happy group. The hope which somehow or the other they lost in the priesthood—or had beaten out of them—has not been revived by departure. To leave the priesthood may not necessarily be a tragedy, but to leave it because of an error in judgment, because of a misreading of the data, is surely a tragedy. Again let me say that I'm making no judgments about individuals, not even to the extent of saying that they have made a mistake personally. But I do find myself wondering if many of them have not been misled by the rather narrow perspectives from which they have been forced to view the problem, or even by certain elements of the Catholic press which have turned the former priest into a folk hero.

I remember appearing on a television program with a man who had left the priesthood and the Church (complete with color motion pictures of his "last Mass" and his "leaving the priesthood" reception—surely an interesting innovation). He assured the rest of us in the program that the Church was going under, that the ship was sinking, and that he was going to get off it before it went under. He insisted that priests were leaving like they had never left before and that they were deserting the sinking ship. None of the rest of us was so unkind as to suggest what kind of creature it is that deserts a sinking ship, though one man did note that the departure rate was not very high. Another pointed out that it was much higher at the time of the French Revolution. The basic difference that I had with this man was not the bad taste of a "leaving the priesthood" reception, or of color motion pictures of his "last Mass," nor even his assertion that priests were deserting the sinking ship in large numbers. I disagreed with his interpretation that the ship was sinking, that the Church, to change the metaphor slightly, was coming apart at the seams. It seems to me from my position on the margins that while the Church is going through a dramatic and at times traumatic change, it is surviving the change better than its has ever survived any major crisis in history. As I said in the last chapter, the root of today's problems is not that there is a waning of enthusiasm about the Church, but that there is more enthusiasm than the present outmoded structures can cope with. I know of no religious movement in history that has come to an end because it had too much enthusiasm.

In many former priests and in many who cling stubbornly to their priesthood too, there is something rather akin to the psychological phenomenon called the panic reaction, a reaction rooted in the primal childhood fear of having

support withdrawn from oneself or, to put it more collo-
quially, to having the rug pulled out from under. The
world in which many priests grew up and were trained,
and the world in which they serve is crumbling about
them; and they almost automatically panic. Life made up
of the Thursday golf game and supper and the summer
vacation with one's clerical cronies, of Forty Hours and
Confirmation dinners, of complaining about the bishop
and the chancery office, a life safe from the people behind
the desk in the rectory office, behind the collar, behind the
confessional screen and behind cliché answers, neat categories and closed worldview is finished. The priestly ministry
centered around wakes, funerals, weddings, athletic programs, periodic condemnation of birth control as the
biggest sin and public high school education as the
biggest problem is dead. The life in which one was always
respected, no matter how abominable one's sermons were,
the life for which most of us were trained and in which
many of us have felt safe and comfortable is no longer
deemed adequate by the younger clergy or by the younger
laity. And this life is being taken away from us.

The patterns of behavior, the roles, the values, the expectations around which such clerical culture was built
were rooted in the immigrant condition of American
Catholicism and the Counter-Reformation condition of the
universal Church. But the immigrant experience is receding
into the past, and the Counter-Reformation is following it.
We are no longer permitted to remain in the warm cocoon
that was so safe and comfortable both physically and
emotionally. We are no longer freed from the necessity
of loving and being loved, of worrying and questioning. We

can no longer overcome occasional bursts of loneliness or boredom in a fever of activity, or in John Barleycorn, or in expensive hobbies, or a collection of large amounts of material possessions. The priesthood was an attractive occupation for some of us because there were not much need to question what we were doing or to think beyond the answers provided by our seminary lecture notes. It was a safe, simple, consoling, respectable life, but it will never be that way again. We may have been trained in the immigrant and Counter-Reformation tradition and lived much of our priestly lives in such a tradition, but now we work in a new Church, thoroughly Americanized and postconciliar. Our Catholic people are well-to-do and reasonably well educated. There has appeared a "psychological generation" of clergy and laity. The theological, liturgical and Catholic action renewals after the Second World War have dramatically changed the image of the priest. Many of the things that we were taught were virtuous (such as keeping ourself safe and secure from the laity) are now thought to be vices. Many of those things that we were taught were vices (such as an opening, questioning, probing attitude about our religion) are now thought to be virtues. The world has been turned upside-down for us, and some of us can't stand the strain.

The suddenness and the drama of this transition has panicked many priests and by no means merely the older ones. Young and old alike, we frequently do not know what we should be doing either in theory or in practice. The props have been pulled out from under us, and the primal panic reaction has reasserted itself. With this reaction comes pessimism and despair. We say that the people no longer respect us, that people are losing the faith and leaving the Church and that celibacy is going. We ask, can I marry? Would anyone marry me? We worry that the Sunday obligation is going, and that means people won't be coming to Mass, and that ruins the parish financial system. The schools are going; everything is going; the whole affair is finished. Let's get out while the getting is good, or let's pull back and hide until the storm blows over. Precise response may be different. One priest may leave, another may hide and burrow himself ever more deeply into the protective care of clerical culture; but the causality is the same. Neither can cope with the confusion, the complexity and the ambiguity of change and of growth.

Under such circumstances of confusion and panic, any crackpot or crank who appears on the scene with a new idea is taken seriously, even though he may have no credentials and no evidence. We are assured that the parish system must go, that vocations are going to dry up, and that we should ordain married men who have jobs and will serve as part-time priests. We are told that the whole ecclesiastical structure is vanishing and that what little work we still feel ought to be done is a waste of time. Most of these analyses and recommendations are false. People are not leaving the Church and the vast majority of priests would not marry even if they could. The parish system may be modified, but in no conceivable future situation is it going to be eliminated. The American Catholic population is not likely to tolerate a merely part-time clergy save as a rare exception. Vocations are erratic, going up in some places and down in others. The Catholic schools will go out of business only if we lose our confidence in them because the lay people have, by and large, retained their confidence in the schools. Change in the nature of the Sunday Mass obligation probably would have no great effect on the Church attendance behavior of Catholics for many decades to come. Even then attendance would probably not become much lower than the Protestant level which is only ten or fifteen precentage points below ours. One could, of course, go on, but it would probably be a waste of time because the panic and the resultant frantic grasping at straws is not the result of careful analysis and will not be refuted by it. Panic results because insecure, rigid and poorly educated men have been able to hide behind a rigidly structured system of certainties. Now the system of certainties has been badly cracked.

I hope I will not be misunderstood. Not all those who are leaving the priesthood are doing so because of the panic reaction, though I think more are leaving for this reason than the Catholic press or priests themselves would be willing to admit. I am saying that among former priests and among those who remain the panic reaction is a powerful force. It is sheer, childish panic that leads us to think the present crisis of change is the death throes of American Catholicism instead of a rich, new beginning. A new beginning, from my perspective on the margins, seems so obvious as to be almost beyond question.

Although our hope must always take root in the Resurrection, there are many social trends at work which seem to make hope particularly relevant at the present time. We have been freed from many of the ideological and organizational inhibitions of the past. We have a glorious opportunity to shape a new, more pluralistic and flexible Church. We can form new relationships with the lay people; we can develop a celibacy which means deeper and richer love rather than sterile bachelorhood; we have the freedom to create more effective forms of education and worship; we live at a time when the world is moving towards the more fully human and more fully Christian life; we can acquire the skills and the knowledge that will enable us to respond more adequately to the religious needs of our people and to form new religious communities in keeping with these needs. The priesthood is being converted into a "career" that is exciting and rewarding and challenging, one which will inevitably appeal to the young. There is great vigor and vitality and enthusiasm in the American Church. Scholarship is still lacking, but imagination, creativity and energy are not. No matter how one looks at it, or at least so it seems to me, the grounds for optimism as well as hope are reasonably strong. Panic and fear are rooted not in reality, but in our personality insecurities and our training. If we have the courage to transcend our timidity and narrowness it seems to me we will quickly conclude that there has rarely been a time when it's been more exciting to be a Catholic priest.

I claim no particular virtue for being able to see things this way. I stumbled into my present outlook point on the margin mostly by accident, and so I was able to escape much of the pain of transition without any conscious planning or effort. I think, however, that I can sympathize with those who are still caught in the old Church. Still little more than an errand boy for a tyrannical pastor or superior, they wonder when all the changes about which everyone is talking will ever have a notable impact on their own lives and work. To these men, I say, the situation in which you find yourself is intolerable, and you have every reason to get out of it. This does not mean that the priesthood is intolerable. Unfortunately, the ones most likely to be caught in the intolerable position are also the ones whose training and temperament makes them least able to take moderate corrective action instead of dramatic, destructive action.

Nevertheless, even allowing for the social, cultural and psychic reasons to explain the panic in the priesthood today, I cannot see why so many older clergy do not understand that the change we are going through is good. Nor do I understand why so many of the younger ones among us do not see that, like all changes, this one must evolve out of the past into the present instead of resulting from a revolution which wipes the slate clean.

We cannot have either the certainty of the dying past or the imaginary future. Therefore, we must exercise restraint to cope with a fluid, dynamic and promising present. Unfortunately, panic is contagious, particularly when it's so hard to get factual information about the dimensions of our present crisis; and when certain segments of the Catholic press, for purposes of their own, enthusiastically whip up feelings of panic and disaster.

The young people are constantly warning each other not to "blow your cool." On occasion the "cool" which is not to be "blown" is a phenomenon which a psychiatrist would call repression. On other occasions it is confidence in emotional maturity in the face of sticky but intriguing situations. Many priests are blowing their cool today, mostly because they refuse to see beyond the stickiness to the interest of their present condition because their hope has always been rigid rather than flexible and because they're not able to "hang loose" and "play it by ear." To paraphrase Gilbert Chesterton slightly, the hotter the situation, the cooler the cleric ought to be. If we can only "cool it" another couple of years, the powerful dynamic at work within the Church will, I firmly believe, cleanse much of the old and the irrelevant out of our system; and we will understand clearly that enthusiasm and hopefulness are much more appropriate responses in the present era in history than anxiety and panic. That it takes effort to stay cool I will not deny, but from my perspective on the margin, the effort seems to be well worth it.

In the final analysis, no one can reassure the priest who is in the process of losing his nerve. No one can persuade the priest who has left that he has made a mistake. No one can persuade the threatened, anxious, panicky priest that his reactions are unrealistic because the behavior of these three different kinds of men is beyond the rational. One must affirm strongly that other reactions are possible, and are more soundly rooted in careful analysis of reality. Only the future can solve the question of whose analysis is right, but out here in the secular world from which I write, there isn't much smart money being bet against the Catholic Church and its priesthood.

[2]
Self-respect

It has taken me some forty years of life to come to the conclusion that I am, after all, a relatively likeable person. Only the Herculean efforts of a number of Catholic friends and the astonishing (at least to me) respect of many non-Catholic colleagues has persuaded me that upon occasion I can even be charming. The really amazing part of this phenomenon is that when one discovers that one is likable, and even upon occasion charming, the level of likability and charm escalates very rapidly, surprising even those who in the face of considerable evidence to the contrary asserted that it was there all along.

Having perused such an offbeat paragraph many, if not most, clerical leaders will respond angrily, "What unmitigated pride! How dare he admit to himself that he can be likable and charming? He's obviously an egotist. Who does he think he is to make himself better than anybody else?"

Such a reaction points up sharply the nature of false humility in the priesthood and the consequent destruction of priestly self-respect. We ought to realize in theory though we don't understand in practice that all creatures of God are likeable, and all of us have the potential for charm. Our refusal to respect and to acknowledge our worth and attractiveness as human beings is in fact an escape—an excuse for withdrawing from human relationships and hiding our tortured insecure little egos behind the smoke screen of false humility. As Karen Horney, a well-known psychologist, has pointed out, the really proud man is the one who sets up impossible ideals for himself, and then, in the light of those ideals, judges himself to be worthless by overlooking what should be obvious: although he's still quite imperfect, he's also very warmly human and far more attractive than the cold inhuman ideal his super ego has set up for him.

It is, therefore, possible to say to any human being, even to a priest, that people will like you if only you are brave enough to put aside some of your defense mechanisms and let them know you as you really are. When someone replies to me, "But it doesn't matter whether people like us or not," I find myself forced to say, "Oh, yes it does. Even though we were trained to say it doesn't, you know better than that."

Self-respect, at least respect for the possibilities of one's self, is absolutely essential for effective relationships with other human beings. Since the priest is a man whose role is primarily relational, he obviously must have a great deal of self-respect. Self-fulfillment or self-actualization has become a battle cry in the present ecclesiastical transition. The pretext that one must fulfill one's self is used as an excuse to leave the priesthood, to miss appointments, to disregard obligations, to ignore instructions, to avoid responsibility. It is the battle cry of the new breed and a dirty word for the old breed. That both groups understand it for the most part in the corrupt version of popular psychology does not seem to be obvious to either side. Self-respect and self-fulfillment are not pretexts. They are obligations. They do not remove responsibilities; they integrate and coordinate responsibilities and impose even deeper obligations to fulfill them.

In the "old Church" or at least in a strong tradition within it, the view of self was summarized neatly by a prayer we used to say in the seminary during the Stations of the Cross on Fridays of Lent, a prayer in which we affirmed and reaffirmed at each station, "I am a worm and no man." One of my contemporaries expressed his objection to such dehumanization by whispering: "I am *not* a worm."

In such a framework self was basically evil even though we prettied up the fact of the evilness of the self by saying it was really deprived rather than depraved. Our life was viewed as a constant battle to eliminate the imperfections in this deprived self. We were taught to view ourselves with distrust, fear and suspicion. Our impulses must be repressed, our affections checked, our tendencies controlled, our impurities washed away by "self-denial." Our vocation was to be "perfect." We were to dedicate ourselves to the arduous and systematic elimination of "imperfection" even to the extent of writing down in our notebook the success or failure of our daily battle against our imperfections. We were urged to ask each other what our predominate fault was, and we discovered that in almost every circumstance our predominate fault was pride.

than by pride. A good deal of this, of course, was silliness
and probably would not have done much harm to a
A few lucky people were more afflicted by "sensuality"
normal, healthy young man. The trouble was that most of
us, like most other middle class American males, were not
normal, healthy young men. We were already considerably
infected by the self-rejection which was endemic in middle
class American society. Furthermore, at that stage of the
game, we did not have enough psychological sophistication
to know that our "predominate" vice was neither sensuality
nor pride. It was self-hatred.

As a result of this enforcement by our training of an
unhealthy tendency already existing in our psychological
background, the situation has arisen where those who
counsel priests, even "normal" priests, are astonished at the
self-loathing, self-repression, self-rejection and self-suspi-
cion that seem to be locked into the priestly personality.
Priests tend to be inhibited, fear-ridden, anxious, uncertain
men who strive to behave quite independently of human
feelings, their own or others, and count themselves virtuous for doing so. Furthermore, people in positions of
responsibility are able to impose on their subjects assign-
ments which are utterly destructive to the personality of
the subjects. They argue that all they are doing is providing the subject with an opportunity to "grow in holiness
and self-denial." Since the self is basically evil, there is no
need to respect its natural tendencies or inclinations, no
reason to suspect that those things which a man would
like to do may also be those which he is best qualified to
do. Certainly, there is no reason to assume that the talents

that a man possesses are a sign from God of what he ought
to be doing.

Both in theory and in practice this view of the human
self is probably heretical. It is surely a sin against the God
who made us who and what we are and who endowed
us with the talents that we have. He who rejects himself
rejects the God who made him, and he who disregards
the talents and inclinations of someone else's personality
disregards the God who created that personality. Modern
psychology substantiates the need to respect one's self
and also to respect the self of others, but we should not
have had to wait for Sigmund Freud and his colleagues to
discover that our approach to human selfhood was danger-
ously sick. Common sense and our own tradition should
have revealed that to us. If the Church abounds in insecure
troubled priests, it is because they were trained to be insecure and troubled. If it abounds in lonely priests, it is
because they were taught that self-imposed loneliness was
the highest virtue. If the Church abounds in amateur priests,
it is because they were taught that it was wrong, or at least
prideful, to want to develop their talents professionally. If
the Church abounds in unhappy priests, it is because they
were victims of the incredible heresy that God did not
want us to be happy.

There is another view of the self more characteristic of
the new Church than of the old and, in my judgment,
equally false. In this view self-fulfillment or doing precisely
what occurs to one at a given moment and abandoning oneself to one's instinctive feelings whatever they happen to
be equals spontaneity. One of the more grotesque manifes-

tations of this is the "spontaneous homily" whether preached by one person or by many. Somehow or other it is assumed that the spirit of God will speak more clearly through us if we don't prepare our remarks than if we do, and that he will speak even more clearly when a group pools its unpreparedness. I am certainly not against the "group discussion homily" particularly when they've been well prepared by all the participants, but it does seem to me to be the most naive kind of nonsense to assume that preparation inhibits effectiveness. (Though, of course, it does for those who don't respect themselves in the first place.)

Among the manifestations of the "spontaneous self" are the "honesty" which masks aggressiveness in a number of the underground ecclesiastical communities, the exhibitionism which is disguised as "relating to people" and the massive lack of discipline and organization, which characterizes the behavior of many young people and not a few older people. Just as the self-rejection of the old Church permitted the superego to reign supreme, so the self-deification of the new Church will permit the id to run unchecked. We don't have to think; we don't have to plan; we don't have to organize; we don't have to be urbane or tactful or discreet. None of these painful human activities are necessary. All we have to be is our "self"— crude, rude, irresponsible, unreliable and incompetent.

There is, as the reader may suspect, a middle way, the way which I, with my social scientific biases, think is based on a realistic appraisal of both the strength and the weakness of the self. In such a perspective, we affirm that the God who redeems is also the God who creates, and that the spirit of God speaks to us, not only through the Scriptures and through the teachings of the Church, but also through what we are. We come from God with nerve endings, digestive systems, brain shape, childhood experience and cultural and ethnic backgrounds. The combinations and permutations of these variables produce a personality that is absolutely unique. There are some things we are really good at, and we really like to do because that is the way we have been made. Therefore, these are the things that we should do even though we may have to undergo considerable training and discipline to become proficient at these things towards which our inclinations lead us.

We are, by the time we arrive in adult life, a more or less integrated system of roles, expectations, norms and values which constitute our personality core (or our identity if you wish). Our essential moral task is to preside over the development of the self, to improve the strengths that we already have and to limit the evil effects of the weaknesses which constrain us. In Professor Abraham Maslow's words:

> . . . our inner nature inasmuch of it as we know so far, seems not to be intrinsically evil, but rather neutral or positively good. What we call evil behavior appears most often to be a secondary reaction to frustrations of this intrinsic nature.
>
> Since this inner nature is good or neutral rather than bad, it's best to bring it out and encourage it rather than to suppress it. If it is permitted to guide our life, we grow healthy, fruitful and happy.
>
> If this essential core of the person is denied or suppressed, he gets sick, sometimes in obvious ways, some-

times in subtle ways, sometimes immediately, sometimes later.

"The inner nature is not strong and overpowering and unmistakable like the instincts of animals; it is weak and delicate and subtle, easily overcome by habit, cultural pressure and any wrong attitudes towards it.

"Even though it is weak, it rarely disappears in the normal person, perhaps not even in the sick person. Even though denied, it persists underground forever pressing for actualization.

Sin then is ultimately self-hatred, the refusal to respect what is good and valuable within us. Those sinful acts which our moral law rejects are above all else a violation of ourselves. The sinner does not love himself enough to be virtuous. It is worth noting, by the way, that I am not equating morality with mental health. I am simply asserting that self-love and self-respect is at the root of all moral behavior, a point which was clearly made in the Scriptures when we were told to love our neighbors as we love ourselves. He who hates and rejects himself is not going to have much to imitate when he tries to love the neighbor the same way he loves himself.

Perhaps an example of the immorality of self-rejection will illustrate my point. Let us imagine a young man who, because of his family training, feels a powerful drive to professional success as a means of self-validation. If he is not a great doctor, or lawyer, or a great business executive, then he will be worthless. So he feels the strong urge to commit himself completely and totally to his career. However, the sexual attractiveness of his wife, the charm of his children, intriguing possibilities of religious commitment, deep fascination of reading, music and the arts, the pleasure of travel and vacation, and the enjoyment of playfulness distract him. The young man hesitates between demands of the career and the demands of this combination of other attractions, and he persuades himself that he cannot have his cake and eat it, too. He cannot be a successful professional and enjoy the other things in life. He feels that professional success is what is really important and what his life is really all about. Therefore, with a superficial show of reluctance, he commits himself irrevocably to his career. Slowly but surely he phases out his interests in the rest of life, persuading himself all the while that this is the most moral decision he could make.

However, from the point of view of this chapter, his behavior is objectively sinful because it is based on self-rejection and self-hatred. If he accepted himself as a valuable and worthwhile human being, he would not *need* professional success as a means of self-validation. He would not feel compelled to *prove* himself by rejecting all the other values in life and all the other inclinations of his own personality simply to respond to one inclination and one obligation. Most of the other "sins" he will commit will flow from this basic self-hatred and self-rejection. Drunkeness, infidelity, hatred, perhaps dishonesty, disregard of his children, his religion and his obligation to grow intellectually are all based on his refusal to establish some social distance between himself and his career as the unique validator of the self.

Obviously, much more could be said about this kind of "immorality" which is rampant in our society. Even in its present sketchy form, the above description provides a good base for comparison of clerical behavior. The priest who permits a very narrow definition of the priesthood and a systematic disrespect for self to inhibit his development is sinning every bit as much as is the businessman, and he will, to the extent of this sin, be an inept and inadequate priest. It would seem that an operation of morality of the self requires: that we respect the self, its talents and its personality core; that we develop the self, use our talents and integrate our personality into a consistent pattern of roles and values and then act according to the principles and beliefs which make explicit these values; that we give the self to others because we recognize that it is something valuable and meaningful to others, even in the face of all its flaws and limitations.

Eugene Kennedy has spoken only half facetiously of the call to imperfection. We don't have to be perfect to love ourselves or give ourselves to others. Granted our faults and frailties and granted the need to better integrate ourselves, there is still no point in calling into question God's good taste in making us who and what we are. The self is on a pilgrimage; it has the basic plan of the pilgrimage in its possession, but it cannot execute the plan without confidence in its own good judgment and the support and love of others. We must respect the essential validity of this plan because it comes from God. We must also maintain a healthy skepticism about the self because it is still a pilgrim, and the complete integration of the value system on the personality core will take place only at the end of the pilgrimage.

Therefore, the critical task of self-fulfillment morality is not satisfying one's instincts, but pushing ahead on the pilgrimage to integration and development. Self-fulfillment consists essentially of responsible behavior, behavior that is responsible to one's own best instincts and also to the rights and the selfhood of those that are around us. We integrate our personalities and continue our pilgrimage essentially by developing our abilities to give ourselves to others responsibly and respectfully, the responsibility and the respectfulness focusing simultaneously on ourself and on the other. There is an interaction between self-respect and respect for others. He who respects himself is at least inchoately able to respect others, and he who respects others develops, by so doing, a respect for himself. Self-fulfillment is anything but spontaneous pleasure-seeking. It is rather the consistent disciplined and orderly attempt to be fully ourselves for others, to be responsible and respectful to them and to ourselves simultaneously. In marriage, for example, self-fulfillment comes not so much from selfishly enjoying the married partner, but rather from responsibly respecting the partner and doing all we can to promote the partner's happiness. Indeed, to the extent that we are not responsible towards our partner in marriage, the possibilities of pleasure and enjoyment are foreclosed. Marriage is self-fulfilling, not because it provides warmth and pleasure, but because it provides an insistent and indeed imperious demand for adult, responsible and respectable behavior.

It has always seemed to me that the basic weakness in James Kavanaugh's approach to marriage is his assumption that instant sex somehow or other is going to be self-fulfilling. It really won't be. Marriage imposes a greater demand for self-discipline and responsibility than does the priesthood. One is not going to enrich his personality by jumping into bed with a woman. While many marriages do contribute to personality development, many others do not precisely because self-fulfillment is equated merely with self-satisfaction and pleasure and is held to be an almost automatic result of the marriage union.

The personality develops in marriage from the constant sacrifice and consideration exercised for the other person, from the adjustment of ourself to the other self in a constant state of dynamic development. The marriage union is a dance in which the two partners gradually learn to adjust themselves to the other's rhythms and, in the process, develop and enrich and improve their own rhythms. It is a difficult and painful and rewarding process reinforced by sexual pleasure which is made far more enjoyable by the ardors of the dance.

We fulfill ourselves either in marriage or out of marriage not by doing what we want to do but by serving others as ourselves. The service of others is difficult but joyful. In marriage it is far more rewarding than sexual intercourse which largely loses its satisfaction, if service for the other is neglected.

[3]
Friendship

It can be taken as axiomatic that man is not meant to be alone. This is true not only reproductively, but economically, culturally and psychologically. We are only persuaded of our own value when there is someone to tell us that we are worth something, to assure us that we matter and that we are important. We cannot be human without friendship because our own self-respect depends upon seeing respect reflected in others. Those of us who hate ourselves refuse to see the respect that others have for us, and then by our behavior preclude the possibility of others seeing anything worth respecting or loving. A friend is one who thinks that we are important as a *person*, not because of what we can do or because of the position we hold.

Loneliness or friendlessness, on the other hand, is the quality of not being important to anyone. There is a considerable amount of loneliness in the life of all too many priests, though this is scarcely necessary. We give up marriage, at least in the present discipline of the Roman Catholic Church, but this does not mean we give up friendship. However, many of us have been taught to behave as though friendships are impossible for priests, save possibly with other priests.

There are still those who would argue that celibacy is not a valid mode of being sexually in the world. After the work of Father Edward Schillebeeck,* Father Eugene Kennedy** and Mrs. Sidney C. Callahan,*** one wonders how they could assert this. If celibacy is a valid mode of being in the world, loneliness is not. Man cannot survive without friends, and a successful marriage must ultimately be a friendship relationship. If one does not marry a friend, or if the marriage partners do not become friends, the sexual magic soon flies away. The root of loneliness for the priest is not that he has no one to sleep with. Many priests would be lonely even in marriage. The real reason why many priests are lonely is that they are not equipped for the friendship relationship.

The root of the friendship relationship is the extraordinarily difficult virtue of trust. If a friend is one who thinks we are important, then trust is a quality that enables us to let ourself be important to others. If we permit trust, then we permit others to make demands upon us. If someone thinks we are important to them, they want us, and we must therefore respond by giving ourselves to them. We must leave ourselves open to them and run the risk that they will take advantage of us, exploit us, "chump us." We must have enough confidence in ourselves that our self-giving will not cause us to lose ourselves but

* *Celibacy* (New York: Sheed & Ward, 1969).

** *Comfort My People* (New York: Sheed & Ward, 1968).

*** *Exiled to Eden* (formerly *Beyond Birth Control*) (New York: Sheed & Ward, 1969), paperback.

rather enable us to find the self even better than that which we have given. We do not hide from our friends nor consider their admiration and respect dangerous. Even though we do not equate trust with either exhibitionism or the destruction of privacy, we trust our friends enough not to be very worried that they may intrude upon our privacy.

Trust sounds quite lyrical when it is being described, but in practice it is extremely difficult. We need only look at a number of marriages which do not seem to have very much of it. Two people live together and breed children and yet spend most of their married life hiding from each other. Physical nakedness is one of the great joys and the great burdens of marriage, but it is both less rewarding and easier than psychological nakedness. The latter is achieved only slowly and painfully, even when the sexual act provides extraordinarily powerful reinforcement for it. The human race is only beginning to learn how to trust and probably will not get very good at it until there is more trust in the marriage relationship. One might add, also, that there will not be much trust in ordinary human relationships until the religious leaders of the people are able to display it in their own behavior.

In a relationship of trust it is not necessary that everything be known about us. The husband need not know everything about his wife (and, if he feels he must, he is likely to be possessive and jealous). But he must know *her*. This means somewhat more than merely being able to predict her behavior.

As I have suggested in another book, marriage is the prototype for human friendships. Friendship, in its turn, is deeply rooted in human sexuality, so all friendships necessarily have a sexual tone to them. It could be said that man has made two great evolutionary leaps in the development of his relationships. He has learned, first of all, that for a creature like himself the mating relationship is ultimately successful only if it is set in the context of friendship and trust. And, more recently he has discovered that this trust which the race has learned can exist in other human relationships between members of opposite sexes or of the same sex. Trust that is the core of friendship is rooted in sexual surrender. Surrender can take place, we have discovered, both inside of marriage and outside of marriage. It need not be oriented toward the generative act, but it is nonetheless irrevocably linked to man's nature as a sexual being. Most human beings are not very good at trust largely because they are not convinced of their own adequacy as human beings, and more specifically, as human beings of their own particular sex. There is still something badly missing in the way we raise children, particularly in middle class American society, so that they grow up feeling sexually inadequate and unsure of their masculinity or their femininity. Under certain circumstances we don't feel that our self is worth knowing or giving, so we develop phony selves behind which to hide without daring to believe that the collection of masks which we present to the world outside is far less attractive than the reality that we are. Self-revelation is painful only because we are afraid that others will not like us, and we desperately hope they will like the masks better than the person we know we are. It might be remarked in passing that one of the most clever of masks is that of pseudo self-revelation, particularly as it is practiced in the cult of raw "honesty" and in some of the so-called "sensitivity" groups.

But if this trust and openness rooted in self-respect and a sense of one's sexual identity is difficult for everyone, it is particularly difficult for priests. The priest dimly perceives that trust is sexual in its roots (though it transcends the genical), and he's been trained through his whole life as a seminarian and a priest to feel that sex is dangerous for him. Even if he hadn't been warned explicitly about the dangers of getting involved with people, he would still be afraid of loosing his celibacy if he became "too friendly" with anyone. The self-loathing and the doubts about one's sexual identity which our childrearing practices produced in most Americans are reinforced in the cleric by his training and ideology. Since he has such little respect for himself and such great fear of his maleness, he cannot expect others to like him, much less to respect him as a man. Therefore, he hides. He builds up a vast and complicated array of defense mechanisms justified by the ideology of "not taking chances" and keeps the world at bay. Alternately, if he decides that he cannot live a lonely life, and no one can, he forthwith concludes that he needs a woman in bed with him and that instant sex will somehow or the other make him a man and a human being. It doesn't, and it can't. But by the time he finds out, he may be psychologically incapable of admitting it to himself and will persistently claim that his loneliness is over, even though he has not changed basically.

Real friendship on the other hand, evolves slowly and requires delicacy, tact, prudence, urbanity and diplomacy. It is patient, that is to say it is based on an evolving commonality which is not at all the same thing as conformity. It is not competitive. We rejoice in the friend's success, for his success is our success. It is open ended. It's always capable of further growth and never satisfied with the state of development. It is outgoing; it does not close in on the community of two. Instead, real friendship opens up both personalities to the whole world around it. And it is pluralistic. The experience of friendship enhances a person's ability to have more friends and his freedom to seek other friendship relationships.

It is, therefore, not a magic answer, not an overnight process and not the linking of genital organs. It is the slow process of giving and receiving, encouraging and reassuring, sharing and growing. It is a process in which through knowing our friends we come to know ourselves. By knowing who and what the friend really is we finally understand who and what we really are. We make the astonishing discovery that we are what we fondly hoped we would be though we never quite believed it possible.

Do priests have friends? Surely they have cronies, but if one looks closely at the bridge clubs or the golf foursomes and views them objectively, one wonders how much friendship there is there. There is affection, certainly, and some concern. Yet these priestly groupings often remind me of teenage cliques—a huddling together of lonely, frightened individuals seeking to survive, eager for social support, yet highly competitive and inhibiting the growth of individual members. So many of the relationships between and among priests are fixated. They stopped evolving long ago during the seminary days. They are harsh and impatient, though they often masquerade under the

cover of noisy camaraderie. They are closed in the sense
that no other reference group is really important to some
members of these priestly cliques. What the other members
of the clique think on any subject from the Vatican Council to the latest movie is all that counts. All basic decisions
are made in the group context, and the individual finds it
very difficult to survive or even be himself outside the
group.

I'm certainly not arguing that there is no friendship
among priests, no trust, no mutual respect. But I think that
friendship, trust and respect are relatively rare in priestly
relationships partly because our training and our life has
kept us immature, suspicious and competitive, and partly
because we are afraid that openness and surrender will
somehow or other reveal us as the worthless people we are
persuaded that we are. I'm inclined to suspect that most
priests who have learned how to trust and to form authentic friendships have learned it in association with lay people
where it is more difficult to hide behind the stylized and
routinized relationships that were firmly fixed in the seminary bull sessions. Not being able to slip quickly into his
stereotyped behavior with some lay people, the priest may
be forced, momentarily at least, to be himself; and he may
make the astonishing discovery that this is infinitely better
than the game he has played with his clerical cronies. At this
point he is likely to become terrified. Maybe he will "fall
in love;" maybe he will "become involved;" maybe he will
"leave the priesthood." These are very real possibilities,
especially when the surroundings of one's priestly life are
virtually intolerable. If one is unhappy as a priest; if one's
ego strength is weak, then the sweet taste of human affec-

tion and friendship may be enough to topple a priestly commitment which is already in serious jeopardy. One will conclude with James Kavanaugh, that one cannot be a man and be a priest.

But those for whom friendship is that serious a danger are very few. Though it may sound harsh at first to say so, they are ill-equipped to be priests, for it is the very nature of the priestly vocation that the priest be a friend to his people. In the words of the Lord, "No longer do I call you servants . . . . But I have called you friends . . . ." John 15:15. The man who incapable of giving himself in friendship is incapable of being an effective priest. The basic problem the Church faces today is that so many priests are afraid of friendship.

If, therefore, there is a risk in opening one's self to others, in slowly tearing down the defense mechanisms and surrendering ourselves to those who would make us important, it is a risk that is not optional for the priest. He cannot be the leader of his people unless, like the Lord, he is their friend. He cannot be their friend unless he gives himself over to them. If he loses himself in this process of giving—and it is to be feared that some have and will— then he did not have the emotional maturity necessary to take on the priestly ministry. It is just as well for him and for the Church that he find another vocation, although he is not likely to be very happy in any other vocation if he lacks a minimum capacity for trust and stability.

It may seem strange that in the early chapters of this book we have argued that trust and self-respect are critical virtues for the priest who wishes to be a creator of the future. Do I consider these the two most important virtues a priest must possess? I would not be inclined to enter into a foolish academic argument about relative importance, but it does seem to me that since, as we will note in the next chapter, the priest creates the future essentially as "an expressive leader", he will not be very successful unless he posses both self-respect and the capacity to trust. An expressive leader without trust and self-respect is the equivalent of a ship captain who does not know navigation or an engineer who does not understand mathematics. The narrow, timid, frightened, insecure, self-rejecting, suspicious priest is a pathetic man. He is a man who needs help, a man who may even have the capacity for growth, but he will not be a creator of the future. We have recruited all too many men of this sort in the priesthood. Then, by their training and by their style of life, we have kept them that way. Even those whose self-respect and trust are further developed have been discouraged in being what they could be and what they ought to be. The picture is not a pretty one, and we would be deceiving ourselves if we thought that the problem is going to be easily solved, particularly without a major reorganization of the structures and styles of the Church.

At the seminary level, things seem to be changing. Apparently different kinds of young people are being recruited and a very different sort of training is provided. Therefore, in the future it seems reasonable to expect that we will have much more confidence and trust in the priesthood even though we may have fewer priests. But what does this say about the present generation, those who are, say roughly between thirty and sixty and who were raised to believe that self-respect was pride, and openness was imprudence? One priest psychologist has suggested to me that little more can be done for this generation but to write it off. While this is surely too grim an analysis, the prospect is not bright. The current cult of sensitivity training has, in my judgment, produced for the most part only more sophisticated and more obnoxious disguises. Psychologists and psychiatrists report that priests are very poor patients because they have a very weak sense of self and because they feel so powerfully guilty over the fact that they need counseling. At precisely the moment, be it an individual or a group therapy session, that the priest is about to become authentically honest about himself (as opposed to the phony exhibitionistic honesty of the group) he is most likely to turn and run, apparently afraid that his prized priesthood is going to be defiled.

I feel uneasy and frustrated every time I attempt to discuss this subject. Confidence and trust are so absolutely essential for a priest but what little we had to begin with was crushed in so many of us by our training and by our life. Now we are told that we must acquire it once again if we are to have any meaning for the Church of the future. We don't know how to do it; we are afraid to try, and we hide from our problems either by denying that they exist or by dismissing the question as being simply "New Breed personalism." That there is much gibberish in the phony personalism of some young clergy and laity is hardly to be doubted, and that self-respect and friendships are imperative in the priesthood is also beyond doubt. To put the matter quite bluntly, there is not nearly enough to go around.

But none of this answers the question of how we are to

get it. Perhaps more positive answers will have to wait the final report of the Commission for the Study of the Ministry and Life of the Priesthood. Until then we must be content with concluding that many, many, many of us need counseling, and the more professional the counseling, the better. This is not to argue that we are sick, but rather that we have latent potentiality for human growth which has been long frustrated. These frustrations prevent us from being happy and from being the kinds of priests the Church needs in its creation of the future. Although the prospect is not especailly bright, we can take some comfort in the wise dictum of the psychologist Nevitt Stanford, "No one is ever too old to grow."

[4]
Leadership

One of the less publicized problems of Catholicism in transition is the parish council. While the existence of such councils receives quite a bit of publicity, and there is new rejoicing in the Catholic press every time a diocese announces the establishment of a system of parish councils, no one has yet had the courage to say in print that our newfound democracy is working very poorly, if at all, in the parish councils. There are a number of reasons for this. Middle class Americans, in particular, tend to generate emotional intensity on political issues in direct proportion to their triviality. They are moderately interested in presidential campaigns, somewhat more interested in gubernatorial campaigns, strongly concerned about local suburban elections and absolutely passionate about neighborhood affairs probably because they have so much money and emotion invested in "protecting" the "good life" that they are attempting to establish for themselves in their local community. People who couldn't care less whether Mr. Humphrey or Mr. Nixon is elected President of the United

States, can be highly incensed at the rerouting of traffic, and they convert lifelong friends into lifelong enemies over the question of whether school is to be dismissed at 2:45 or 3:00 P.M. Something about local politics, particularly when it is affiliated with the Church, draws the kooks out of the woodwork. The frustrated, the malcontent, those who have little power influence in any other part of their lives are the ones most likely to become involved in church work and most likely to be active in the emerging parish councils. They have refined the standard paranoid style of American politics to a new peak of perfection in parish councils. Democracy in the Church is as old as the Church, but it hasn't been practiced much in recent years, and the styles and techniques of civilized, democratic discourse are being learned very painfully by all involved. The clergy is afraid that someone is trying to take power away from them, and the laity is equally afraid that the whole thing is a game in which they're being manipulated by the clergy. Finally, the internal conflicts between pastor, assistants and sisters lead to each seeking support in factions of the parish council so that the disagreements among the parish staff are now written large throughout the whole community.

These agonies of emergent democracy are about what can be expected as we go through the painful process of learning or relearning how men govern themselves in trust and respect. In addition to the problem of learning the basic skills of civil democratic discourse, there remains the somewhat painful question of what the priest ought to be doing while the battles rage within the parish council, particularly since the priest feels that much of his power is being lost to the emerging council. The council enhances; it does not weaken the priest's power. To explain why this is so we must take a close look at the priest's role as leader in the contemporary Church.

Sigmund Dragastin, a noted priest-psychologist, has very felicitously described the priest as "the expressive leader" of the Christian community. This phrase sums up, at least for the social scientist, many different ideas about the proper priestly role. (I should emphasize that in the rest of this chapter, I am merely using Doctor Dragastin's phrase as a jumping-off point, and he is not to be blamed for the interpretation that I put upon his words.) An "instrumental" leader is one whose primary concern is with getting things done, the fulfillment of tasks, organization, administration, implementation. He is a doer, a planner, a decision maker. The expressive leader, on the other hand, is more concerned with both the "big picture" and with the people in a group. He makes sure that the visions of the community are clear and that the morale of its members is high. He soothes over hurt feelings, reassures the troubled, encourages the weary, makes peace between the angry and inspires the discouraged. In Western culture, through what is probably a major aberration, we have tended to let the husband become the instrumental leader of the family and the wife the expressive leader. However, recent psychology suggests that in the healthiest families the wife is more instrumental and the husband more expressive. In our business enterprises generally we have also given the top role to the instrumental executive, the man who gets things done. Once again modern research shows that in the large complex organization things aren't going to be done very well unless the goals of the organization are symbolically embodied in an expressive leader who is also concerned about the morale of the organization's members. In other words, in the modern complex corporate body the expressive leader is more important than the instrumental leader.

Ideally, of course, one man or one woman can play both roles. The Kennedy family, for example, seems to have produced a number of people who are not only terribly effective administrators, but who also have the charisms that can move the minds and hearts of men. Similarly, the great college presidents combine the administrative talent with expressive abilities. However, it is not absolutely necessary that one person possess both talents, and probably it should not be expected of most of us. Pope John was far more successful at the expressive role than the instrumental one. Hence, we rate him as the most important pope in the modern world and also, be it noted, the most effective. Furthermore, administration is becoming more and more of a technique, and administrative skills can be delegated either to machines or to technically trained personnel. The Church, the nation, the university, even the automobile company ought not to have to worry about administration since there are available in our society the trained technicians who can handle administrative responsibility. The truly effective leader in the complex and confused corporate structures of the modern world is the one who can inspire men, who can move their minds and hearts, who can see great visions and who can encourage people to believe in themselves, their talents and their community. The pope, the president, the bishop, the priest who is concerned about effective leadership of his people must, therefore, concentrate heavily on the expressive dimension of his role. Unfortunately, most of us have been trained to think of the priest, and particularly the pastor, as a man who administers, one who gets things done, rather than a man who encourages, inspires and loves. The instrumental leader is a man who *does*. The expressive leader is a man who *is*. The world and the Church today need men who *are*.

I'm not suggesting that the priest should be shorn of all administrative functions, but I am saying that administrative functions are those that can be most effectively delegated and also most effectively placed under the supervision of committees, the parish council or diocesan pastoral councils. But you cannot inspire and reassure by committee. You cannot love by committee. You cannot move the minds and hearts of men by committees. These goals are all the result of interpersonal behavior. To be a success at interpersonal behavior, you must first be a person.

I suspect some hardnosed clerics will dismiss this as pious sentimentality and will accuse me of reducing the role of the priest to that of a morale officer. There is some strange quirk in our American consciousness which makes males feel insecure and somewhat less male if they are not administrators, if they are not *doing* things. It is difficult for me to see how Pope John or John F. Kennedy, or the President of Notre Dame University can be dismissed as morale officers. Yet their major contributions have not been administrative, but inspirational, one might even say, prophetic. The priest is a poet and a prophet embodying in his own life and in his own pattern of relationships the vision which he sees. By the kind of person he is, he inspires men and women to follow him on the pilgrimage of the people of God.

Some young people reacting, I suspect, to the sometimes demented search for "relevance" which they observed in some of their clerical contemporaries, have pointed out to me that a priest really ought to be useless and irrelevant. It seems to me that they are saying in somewhat different and perhaps more striking language what Doctor Dragastin says when he argues that the priest must be an expressive leader. They are not opposed to priests marching on picket lines, demonstrating for peace, or even, heaven save us, working in social science research centers. They are saying that what is important about a priest is not what he does but the quality and style of his life and his behavior, in other words, *who* he is. His essential priestly task as a leader in the community is to move the minds and hearts of men. This is not done by performing specific acts, but by the loving quality of his relationships and by the vision of life which he embodies in these relationships. The priest who marches on picket lines or demonstrates for peace may be very relevant, but if he does not have the spark of human goodness and love which draws people after him, then he is after all, sounding brass and tinkling cymbals. As the modern Calvinist industrialist judges it, the expressive leader, the morale officer, the poet, the seer of visions, the lover are irrelevant and useless. They are not *doing* anything. The younger clergy who are madly seeking for relevance may be assuring themselves of their own Calvinist masculinity, but they ignore the old Christian and pagan tradition of the priestly role. In their eagerness to do what everybody else does they fail to do that which only they can do.

As we've said before in this book, the priest creates the future essentially by facilitating the improvement of the quality of human relationships, and to do so he must be a master of relationships. He must be able to reassure, to radiate confidence in times of difficulty and confusion, to prophesy when the vision grows dim and the hearts grow cold, to be concerned over the troubled and the afflicted, to share in the emotionality of the joyous and the enthusiastic, to bring together both people and ideas and see the world conjunctively rather than disjunctively. He must be loyal, generous, hopeful and joyous, playful and merry. The administrator answers questions; the expressive leader asks them. The administrator tells people what to do; the expressive leader challenges them to do the best which is in them. The administrator lays down the law; the expressive leader stirs up the heart. I repeat, both are necessary. The priest to some extent must do both, but the expressive role is the essential and predominant one. The emergence of parish councils should free the priest to play the expressive role more frequently and more fully and, hence, considerably enhance his power with his people.

Whenever I say these things to priests, someone is bound to rise up and say you can't expect that from all of

us because we don't have the kind of personality to influence other people. But what kind of personality is
needed? One does not have to be a Pied Piper or a natural
charmer to move other men. On the contrary, one's leadership is likely to be more effective if one has to put effort
into playing an expressive or prophetic role. Neither the
late President Kennedy nor his brother were naturally
charismatic men. The President was reserved and aloof, the
Senator shy and somewhat timid; but because of their
fierce intellectual conviction of their mission in life, they
were able to move the minds and hearts of many Americans
as few people ever have in the nation's history. Pope John's
charm can be found in one variety or another, one imag-
ines, in thousands of elderly Italian clerics, but he was the
first one in a long time who had the nerve not to permit
his charm to be swallowed up by the pomp and trappings
of the papacy. There may be a few of us who are quite
incapable of influencing others, but if we are, we are sick
and badly in need of psychiatric help. Most of the rest of
us do have some latent expressive ability and probably
more impact on people than we're willing to confess to
ourselves. It's not a question of acquiring a talent we do
not have, but rather of developing an incomplete talent
that we're hiding from ourselves out of fear and diffidence.
There is no single mandatory style of expressive leadership.
President Theodore Hesburgh of Notre Dame and former
President Michael Walsh of Fordham University are both
masters of it. Yet they are very different kinds of men.
Some expressive leaders are quiet; some others are dynamic,
and even, on occasion, noisy. Some are soft sell, and some

are very high pressure. The Lord, wise creator that he is, has put as many different styles of expressive leadership in the world as there are human beings. It is not necessary for us to imitate anyone else. All we have to do is to express that which is best in ourselves, as frightening as this prospect may seem to us.

I was certainly persuaded as a younger priest largely by the quality of my seminary training and of seminary friendships that I had no talent in dealing with people and would have almost all my influence as a priest on the levels of ideas and values. Having operated this way for ten years, particularly with young people, I one day made the astonishing discovery that most of the young people who stayed around did so, not because they agreed with my ideas or even understood them, but because they liked me. I still don't quite understand why, and the realization was one of the most terrifying experiences of my life. I will also confess that I've grown rather to like it. As a seminarian and a young priest I would have said, dutifully repeating the spiritual directors of our seminary, that is was wrong for people to like their priest because that would interfere with them loving the God for whom the priest was suppose to be a mediator. Even then it should have been clear to me how absurd this was. How else are the people to know God unless they can know him through the personality of his mediator? I would say now that the goal is surely not to persuade people to like you. The goal is to be true to that which is best in you even though you be terribly insecure about it. Then you can assume quite as a matter of course that they, or at least those among them with good taste, do like you. Surpisingly enough, this apparently arrogant approach really requires a great deal of humility, and it is extraordinarily effective.

I am not suggesting, heaven save us, that we manipulate the affections of our people. Group dynamics, sensitivity training and other developments of modern psychology can be quite useful in the work of the priest, but they are no substitute for love or trust. Often they become a blind for covert aggression. Our current crop of "groupists" drift from one kind of psychological gimmick to the other, thinking that eventually they will find something that will enable them to be effective priests. I fear they are very much missing the point. The something that must be found is inside one's self, a faith in the vitality of the message that one has to bring and the validity of the self as a bearer of the message. The priest who is conscious of the tremendous personal influence he has on his people must be wary of using that influence. He must be conscious of how easy it would be for him to slip over into the manipulation of the affections and the emotions of those who look to him for inspiration. But, because the danger of manipulation is present, the priest is no more excused from playing an expressive role than he is excused from trust because the danger of losing celibacy is present in trust. There is, if the truth be told, considerable danger in getting out of bed in the morning.

I have chosen to use in this chapter, and to some extent in previous chapters, the language of behavioral science and existential philosophy, but I trust it will be obvious that the ideal of the priesthood that I am describing is not

something new. One need only look at St. Francis of
Assisi, Ignatius of Loyola, Vincent DePaul, Benedict,
Augustine and Gregory to see that great things are almost
always done by expressive men. I am merely suggesting in
somewhat different language that we ought to be all the
things that the best of the traditional spirituality said we
should be. But we should be them with the emotionality,
love, confidence, self-respect and trust that our Cartesian
training and ideology have almost squeezed out of us. We
will create the future essentially through the quality of
our relationships. Anything else that we may engage in
may be admirable, but it is also beside the point.

On a priests' retreat I gave recently, a group of young
people gave brief talks each evening. The clergy were fully
prepared for what they often hear from lay people speaking
on retreats: criticisms of their failures and a demand for
more lay rights. I think that if this had been the message
of my young friends there wouldn't have been any surprise
or any discomfort. Priests are used to being castigated in
the contemporary American church, and they are better
at castigating themselves than other people are. But what
the young laity said was quite different. They told the
priests that they liked priests; they needed them; they
wanted their leadership; and they wanted their priests to
love them in a warm and human way. They assured the
retreatants that inspiration, affection, concern and love
were the most important things the priest could bring to
his people.

The retreatants, to give them due credit, were charmed
by the young people and very courteous to them, but

they were profoundly skeptical. First of all, the unanimity of the message led the priests to suspect that I had put my friends up to saying the same thing. (I am quite capable of this kind of chicanery, but in this particular instance, I didn't). Second, they argued that such intensely dedicated young Catholics who demanded loving relationships with their priests were obviously not typical. (In many ways my friends were not typical, but that which they were demanding of their priests is typical of a very large number of the best of the younger generation of Catholics.) Finally, the priests suggested in the question period that they really couldn't afford to be deeply involved emotionally with their people because it might be a threat to celibacy, and because there were so many people in a parish that they couldn't love all of them equally. (This response made my young friends shake their heads sadly. Obviously, the priests hadn't understood what they were talking about.)

The young lay people were surprised by this reaction. They had come to praise priests, to reassure them, to encourage them, to tell them that they were important. But this message seemed to frighten the retreatants. It made them defensive and insecure. As one seventeen-year-old said to me, "Why don't they want to believe that they're important to us? Why don't they want to believe that we would like to be able to love them?" I suppose there are many answers to her question, but the two that were most appropriate come almost at the same time: "They were afraid to believe it", and "It was too good to be true."

Because it is too good to be true, we continue our search

for relevance, or for efficient administrative techniques, or for methods of group manipulation which excuse us from the obligation of being useless, irrelevant, and inexpressive. We would rather be half human than more human; we would rather keep people at bay than have them flocking around us; we would rather hold ourselves as passive conduits of the grace of the Holy Spirit than as active cooperators. Indeed, it is all too good to be true.

[5]

Sensuality

The reader may get the impression that I was a frustrated and unhappy seminarian back in the late 40's and early 50's and that I am taking out many of my frustrations against those who trained us in the seminary. In truth, I was a quite happy and well-adjusted seminarian, and I became angry at our training only after ordination revealed to me how inadequate it had been. Nor am I necessarily critical of the men who gave us our training. By the traditions that they understood, by the values of their own particular times, they were good and dedicated priests. The mistakes that were made with us and the heavy bonds that still lie upon us even today were mostly social, structural and cultural rather than personal ones. But there was no word in the vocabulary of the seminary directors that was more ugly than the word "sensuality." Indeed, it was usually said with such horror as to sound positively lascivious. To be "sensual" was almost as bad as to be an "animal", and to be an "animal" was just about as bad as anyone could be. Looking back on those days it is hard for me to understand how even then we could have believed them, or they could have believed themselves. Granted that it might be easy to misunderstand and misinterpret St. Paul about the battle between the flesh and the spirit, it still is extraordinarily difficult to see how both our directors and we ourselves could overlook the rest of the Catholic philosophical and theological tradition which vigorously affirms that the human body and the human senses are good, and that the delights of the senses and the pleasures of the body are in no sense evil.

I think that at the present time it is possible to go beyond merely the assertion that sensual joys are perfectly legitimate for man and to assert that a well-developed sensuality is a positive benefit. Indeed, it is an indispensable resource to effective priestly work.

This chapter is much more speculative than most of the rest of the book and lest I be misunderstood, let it be clearly noted that it is exploratory. I intend to raise certain issues and to open certain questions, some of which may seem shocking. But none should be interpreted as providing definitive answers, much less suggesting practical courses of action.

I would define sensuality as the quality of being attuned to the activity of our senses, and particularly of our feeling flesh, our eyes and our ears. I presume the sensuality of which I am speaking is *responsible* in the sense that *responsible* has been used in previous chapters, that is, that our attunement to the life of the senses takes place in a context of our responsibility to ourself and to others and with a full realization that sensuality, like trust and affection, can through either malice or misunderstanding be misused and abused. I cannot agree with those who think that the possibility of a misuse of some precious human characteristic permits us to attempt to blot that characteristic out of our lives. Indeed, it would be a pretty good trick to be able to blot the senses out of our lives.

Let me note further that my exploratory speculations are inspired in part by the signs of revolt against Cartesian rationalism which we see all around us. (Generally speaking, one hears that the revolt is against Aristotelian rationalism, but why in heaven's name poor Aristotle should be accused of trying to separate the intellect from the emotions is something I've never quite been able to understand. René Descartes, who thought of us as spirits imprisoned in flesh, is surely the guilty party.) The hippies, experimentation with drugs, psychedelic art, musical groups such as the Beatles, Acid Rock and other rather strange developments of the old blues and rhythms, the new interest in astrology, palmistry, and even diabolism, the popularity of Indian gurus who sound suspiciously like John of the Cross or Ignatius of Loyola, the tremendous surge of interest in fairy stories of the Tolkein variety are manifestations of disenchantment with today's world. Even the romantic anarchism of some student radicals seems to me to point to restlessness and dissatisfaction with our rationalistic, scientific, computerized, organized, modern world that ignores or pronounces irrelevant the human senses, human emotions and human passion. The nonrational in the human personality is ignored or repressed only at the risk of having it reappear as irrational. To put the matter somewhat differently, we ignore the demonic in us only at the peril of having it reappear as the diabolic. A total surrender of reason to passion is as bad as a total repression of passion by reason, and the latter usually generates the former.

I have no objection to the hippies' prescription of "tuning out" to "turn on." I interpret it to mean breaking out of the narrowly rationalistic hyperorganized life we ordinarily live to allow free rein to the nonrational elements that are part of us. My quarrel with the hippies is that one should not need drugs to "tune out" and to "turn on," and that one must not give up reforming the Calvinist, industrial society to make room in it for emotionality, sensuality and laughter. Finally, I disagree with the hippies and all their relatives (even though I've come to like some forms of the new art and the new music) to the extent that they think that emotionality and sensuality can be acquired by "blowing their minds." I take this to mean pretty much an abandonment of reason. It would seem, on the contrary, that we can give ourselves over to a life of the senses, to emotionality, to passion with safety and security only when reason is hovering in the background and providing the context for our sensuality. Otherwise, it seems to me sensuality ceases to be responsible and moves from the demonic to the diabolic. The hippies and their ilk go to the opposite extreme from our seminary directors. The latter didn't want us to be animals while the former would prefer that we were not *rational* animals. Stuffy old Aristotelian that I still am, I must say that human happiness consists of a balance of animality and rationality, a flexible balance which can shift and adjust so that it is appropriate to a given situation. In the height of passionate lovemaking husband and wife transcend reason, but this does not mean that their behavior is irrational. Similarily, the mystic lost in contemplation is nonrational but not irrational. On the other hand, the harried businessman at an evening concert worrying about the next day, or justifying the concert on the grounds that during the intermission he will see a client may be behaving quite rationally, but also very inhumanly.

It is quite clear that the nonrational as a modality of communication has been sadly neglected in our Calvinistic industrial world—whether it be the suprarational of contemplation and meditation, or the infrarational of sensuality and emotionality. Unfortunately, the Catholic Church has not notably resisted this hyperrationalizing tendency of the industrial society. Indeed, the Church has permitted itself to become in some countries almost as Calvinistic as the Puritans. How a religion which produced Francis of Assisi and Meister Eckhart can ignore the nonrational is difficult to understand. But we certainly have ignored it. To make matters worse, we have so academicized mysticism and contemplation with our elaborate talk about the various "ways" that we have frightened many of our people away from what is ordinary human behavior.

It's a risky business because Kantianism, Calvinism and scientific rationalism all create a fear of losing absolute control, a fear which in some sort of weird self-fulfilling prophecy actually generates loss of control. The Protestant ethic may, as Max Weber put it, lead to the capitalist revolution. It also has led to Haight-Ashbury. (I am well aware that the hippies deserted Haight-Ashbury for other more remote places such as the Big Sur and Mount Shasta. I use the term symbolically, not geographically.)

The priests, as creators of the future, shapers of human relationships and expressive leaders of men must be in tune with their senses, their emotions, their animality without either fear or presumption. The priest must understand the rhythm of life, and of his life, the attractiveness of the world of the senses and the attractions of his senses; he must discipline and focus his sensual activity so that it is responsible both to his own personhood and to the personalities of others. He must respect his own sexuality, not merely as something that is good in itself, but as a mode of being in the world and a mode of communicating with others that is valid and has nothing to do necessarily with being married.

To put the matter somewhat differently, the priest ought to be able to view his sexuality not only as something that is good in itself and valuable to itself but also as something that is a positive asset to his work. There is a very sensitive "chemistry" in communication between the sexes which operates at the intuitive and the emotional level and which consequently enriches human relationships and makes them more effective, particularly if we allow ourselves to be conscious of the operations of this "chemistry" and the messages it bears. A number of psychologists point out that in many counseling situations it is extremely helpful if the counselor is of a different sex from the client because, at least in the present development of human culture, it seems that communication across sexual lines is richer, deeper and more informative—for those willing to listen—than it is between members of the same sex.

Such a comment in some clerical circles would lead to snide laughter, leering and double meaning comments. Such immaturity can be dismissed. If we stop to think for but a moment, it becomes clear to us that nonverbal communication between a man and a woman has far more emotional overtones than most nonverbal communication between two men or two women. This is as it should be, and it would be rather odd if it were any different. In conversation with a woman, a man, at least an ordinary man, is more alert, more sensitive, more perceptive, and if the truth be told, more interested than if the conversation were with another man. Similarly, a woman is, all other things being equal, far more open to influence by a man than she is by another woman. My masculine bias, I suppose, led me to choose the statement of roles in the last two sentences. Obviously, the exact reverse of the assertions of the last two sentences is also true. A man is more likely to be influenced by a woman, and a woman is more sensitive and perceptive in a conversation with a man. It ought to follow from this that priests would be more effective in their work with women than with other men, and they should more readily play the role of expressive leaders for women than they do for men.

It is necessary to add two clarifications to protect me from superficial responses of clerical reviewers. I am not asserting that priests should work only with women or that their work with men is doomed to ineffectiveness. I am saying that because in many ways a woman is a more pleasant partner than a man, work with her should be easier.

None of this is particularly revolutionary or surprising until we look at the reality. Instead of being more effective with women, priests are less effective. They are afraid of women, particularly when the women are sexually attractive, and particularly when a sexually attractive woman is also intelligent. The normal reaction of priests when faced with any kind of a relationship with an intelligent and sexually attractive woman is fear and then repression of his instincts on the grounds that this is the only way to be "safe." Sometimes it turns out that repression isn't safe because, if instincts are repressed enough, they may break out somewhere else in line with the old Irish political dictum, "the bigger they come, the harder they fall." Even if repression is effective, it does not mean that it's either wise or human. Safeguards ought to come from the reality of relationships, the consideration of who the priest is, and who the woman is, and what their proper relationship to each other ought to be. If safety does not come from this reality, then there probably ought not be any relationship with women, and the priest in question might seek for himself a suitable monastery. A wife would be no solution because the man in question would then have to face the fact that the marriage bed does not make other women unattractive.

The sparkle in a woman's eye, the flash of her smile, her soft laughter, the curves of her body, the warmth of her person were designed by Providence to be disconcerting and fascinating to men. They are not designed, certain Fathers of the Church to the contrary, to bring men down to perdition. This attraction is also a channel for communication, understanding and sympathy. The priest who is sensitive to the nuances of this communication will be not a poorer priest, but a better priest and a better human being. That there is in this fascination the possibility of some unease and what we used to call in the old days, temptation, is not to be denied. Although the priest who is practiced in the virtue of sensuality is not afraid of his impulses and does not feel the need to repress them or deny them completely, neither is there any reason why he should think that he is a slave to them and that he cannot keep them reasonably well ordered in the context of responsible reality. If he can't in this day of mini skirts, he would be well advised not to walk down State Street or Michigan Avenue or the equivalents of those streets anywhere else in our country.

In other words the priest must be sensual enough to enjoy women, their faces, their bodies, their laughter and their charm, realizing that in such enjoyment there is not necessarily either perdition or salvation, but rather the possibility of friendship, affection and intelligent, meaningful human relationships. Because he permits himself to enjoy women, he's better able to understand them, to help them and encourage them on their pilgrimage, and at the same time receive their help in his efforts as a leader of the Christian people. For the priest not only teaches his people, he learns from them. And it seems very likely that he has more to learn from the women who are on the pilgrimage with him than he has from the men.

I don't know what the preceding paragraphs do to the old practice of "custody of the eyes" which was urged upon us at the seminary, but I have a rather strong hunch that it was not practiced much anyhow. At least I hope that "custody of the eyes" was not taken too seriously by most seminarians.

There is also a sexual element in the relationships between priests and other men, but our society has made very little progress in understanding the impact of sex and the relationship between men. About all we are able to do on this subject is to make tawdry jokes about homosexuality. However, I think it is obvious enough that in friendship among males who are heterosexual there is an element of sexual attraction that is both inevitable and healthy. I feel unqualified to describe it, much less to suggest its implications for the life of the priest, though it is a question which ought to be kept open and which ought to be investigated.

I trust that no one will say that because I am advocating greater trust, confidence and enjoyment in relationships between priests and women that I necessarily am arguing against celibacy. On the contrary, this entire chapter is written within the context of an assumed celibate priesthood. It is romanticism to think that marriage of itself enables a man to be open, relaxed, sensitive and enjoying in his relationships even with his wife, much less with any other woman. The problem is not so much with what Professor Kinsey used to call sexual "outlets" but with confidence in one's own sexuality, a confidence which marriage may enhance if one already has it, but which marriage will not create if one lacks it.

The sensuality of the priest is, of course, not limited to his dealings with members of the opposite sex, pleasant as such dealings may be. It is quite incredible how little we hear or see or taste or smell in our mechanized industrialized society. We bemoan the fact that the machines are dehumanizing us. If they are, it is because we let them. The priest, of all people, should have the best reasons for not permitting himself to be turned into a computer card. Furthermore, there is no opposition between sensuality and contemplation as our seminary spiritual directors may have led us to believe. The experience of St. Francis of Assisi shows that the man who can take time to be attuned to his senses, and who makes this attunement habitual is also able to contemplate the data which his senses have brought to him. He who is attuned to the world is also attuned to the Creator of the World. The suprarational and the infrarational are intimately connected, and the man who in the context of rational understanding permits himself to feel at home with his sensuality will also be skillful at feeling at home with his mysticism. The new world which the Church and its priests are striving to create will never be a world in which all the various dimensions of the human personality are in perfect harmony. Nonetheless, it is possible that when we come to understand more and more of the human personality a great deal of the discord and disarray that presently afflicts us can be eliminated. The compulsive, Calvinistic fear of loss of rational control is something that we can easily dispense with, and if the priest is a Calvinist, suspicious of his senses and afraid of women, he can hardly expect his people to be any better.

[6]

Hilarity

There is more to the Camelot myth as it is associated with the Kennedy family than sentimentality. Camelot represents a new and distinctively Catholic element in American culture and one that suggests certain important lessons for the church and its priests.

A number of different myths about the United States turn up in literary and political writings of our republic, particularly in the most fascinating of literatures, the inaugural addresses of the presidents. America is a new Rome, complete with its classical Capitol and its somewhat frightening dedication to the noble, reserved, dignified, sober, farseeing virtues of the citizens of the Roman republic. Its most noble, reserved, dignified, and farseeing public officers are called Senators. Some newspapers describe the Senate as a "tribune." It is also thought of as a new Eden, a rich and abundant garden, a material and human paradise in which men built a new civilization in a new world. Finally, it's frequently described as a new

Israel where new chosen people settling in a new land flowing with milk and honey have set out on a new Messianic mission to save the world.

Once one grants that all myths are exaggerations, but that they serve as important symbols around which we can focus our goals and values, these three myths are worthy and reputable ones. They are also woefully serious and sombre, particularly when they are expressed, as they most frequently were, in the context of Calvinistic thinking in 19th century American society.

I trust our brothers will not be angry at me when I say that the American myths are essentially Protestant of the rather puritanical variety.

In contrast, Camelot is unassailably Catholic. Whatever roots the legend may have in the pagan nature religions, the myth is quite Catholic in the form it has been passed down to us. Even in C. S. Lewis' modern version, Merlin speaks Latin and announces on arrival that he is very definitely a Christian, and that those who signed him up to work for the other side have made a horrendous blunder.

Even though it is fully aware of the implications of the tragic, Camelot is a merry place with its multi-colored pennants dancing merrily in the brisk spring winds, its brave and courtly men and its beautiful music, story telling and laughter. Its knights realize that eventually they will die, and the women know that they must suffer, but they are not afraid. The inhabitants of Camelot do not run away because the sense of the tragic does not take away their vision, a vision which leads their most noble knights to go off and seek the Holy Grail.

Camelot is a myth of joy and laughter because it is a Christian myth. It believes in the Resurrection—the return in triumph over death. Ethel Kennedy makes her astonishing walk on the funeral train because she is very much a woman of Camelot.

I would argue that one looks in vain in the American culture to find previous examples of the Camelot style. I would further argue that it is no mere accident that the Kennedys brought the Camelot myth into American life. They were not only Catholic, but Irish Catholic. One is reminded of the ancient story about the Irishman and the Englishman who were drinking toasts in a public house in Dublin. The Englishman drank a toast "to England where things are always serious, but never desperate." The Irishman responded with a toast "to Ireland where things are always desperate, but never serious."

Belloc was wrong when he expressed his conviction that laughter, like wine, could be found wherever the Catholic sun would shine. There are, it is very much to be feared, many Catholic places where there is neither laughter nor good red wine nor much sun either. Nonetheless, the point of the Camelot message is well taken. Persons who believe in the Resurrection ought to be joyous people, and Catholic Christians who take a relatively more benign view of their nature than our separated brothers ought to be a more joyous, cheerful and playful collection of people. To the extent that they are sober, grim and dour, they fail as Catholics. The Camelot myth came along at just about the right time in American society because we have progressed just about as far as we can with the somber myths of the past. If the problems we face can be resolved, it will only be because we have been able to capture the humor, the wit and the playfulness of the Camelot attitude. If Catholicism has a major contribution to make in the development of the American culture, it is to add playfulness, merriment and wit to a society that takes itself too seriously.

If Catholics are the ones who are to bring hilarity into American life, it will be through the playfulness of their relationships with one another. Priests ought to be the most hilarious of all. They are the ones who are the masters of human relationships with the Church and hence masters of hilarity. Yet, American Catholics are not particularly hilarious, and the clergy and the hierarchy are not exactly the type of people one would invite to a party in the certainty that in their presence the party could not fail.

The phrase, "celebrate Mass," is, I am sure, unconsciously ironic. We've heard it so often that we are unaware of how little like a celebration the typical Sunday Mass really is and how very little like a celebrant most of us priests really are. The clergy are, in the devastating words of the young, "party poopers."

What do we have to celebrate? It seems to me that there are two things we are celebrating: life and unity. And modern man desperately wants to celebrate both. We who are Catholics believe that Christ's Resurrection brought all mankind life and unity, and that the Resurrection continues in time and space through the Church and we believe that the Eucharist unites all men with another. We are the ones who have the most to celebrate, yet we find it very difficult to be celebrants.

Yet the situation is changing. Two years ago two

colleagues and I made a grand tour of American Catholic higher educational institutions for the Carnegie Foundation. We were appalled at the abysmal state of campus liturgy. But this past year on revisiting some of the schools, I was amazed to see the transformation. Some disregard the chancery offices, but the old liturgy was old, drab and anything but celebrating, and the new liturgy was alive, imaginative and joyous. It did, indeed, celebrate; and it did, indeed, bring young men and women together in rejoicing union. The results of the change were even more astonishing than the change itself. At the same time that many other indicators of religious activity were falling in the Catholic population, daily Mass attendance had skyrocketed at those colleges and universities where the new liturgy was in vogue. I suspect that large numbers of these young people are going to demand joyous liturgical celebrations in their parishes in years to come. They will also demand joyous celebrants. They should make such demands for it is their right to do so.

In another book* I have described how the liturgy is sacred play, a make-believe "game" that men go through in order to affirm their unity in the material world around them, with their fellow men and with their God. When playfulness goes out of liturgy, it becomes ritualized and ultimately meaningless. The Byzantine court ritual of the old Roman solemn high Mass was playful at one time (despite the serious mask which we often wear over our playfulness). But such a form of ritual playfulness went out of fashion, probably by 1789.

* *Religion in the Year 2000* (New York: Sheed & Ward, 1969).

However, the important point of this chapter is not that our liturgy ought to be truly a celebration, but rather that our liturgists ought to be truly celebrants—hilarious, merry men whose whole ministry is characterized by playfulness. I'm not suggesting, God protect us, that we should all strive to be hail-fellow-well-met, bouncy Friar Tucks, Bing Crosbys or pleasant Irish elderly monsignors of so many Hollywood productions—though I don't reject the playfulness of any of these personality types, either.

There are some of us whose glands, circulatory, respiratory and digestive systems incline us to have somewhat more sanguine dispostions than others. I, for one, am not particularly predisposed to be playful, and I have a built-in inclination to find parties unmitigated bores. On the other hand, I can, with some effort, work up the spirit of playfulness without substantial assistance from artificial means.

But the question is not whether we are naturally merry or naturally morose. Our religious commitment makes us hopeful. This hope must be integrated into our behavior and generate the style of playfulness which is in keeping with the rest of our personality. Yet, most of us priests are not very good at it. Our senses of joy are inhibited by our puritanism; our ability to relax is restricted by the structure of our lives and the fear of "letting go of ourselves." We have been warned of the need for "reserve" and the dangers of "worldliness." Although we believe in the Resurrection, our belief is apparently not strong enough to overcome the weaknesses of our personalities or the ideological blinders that our training has rigidly fixed on our heads.

I am suspicious of the priest who must constantly be asking himself whether he is happy. If the question comes up frequently, he is not. If a priest is unhappy, the problem is usually in the internal environment, not in the external one. If the external environment deprives us of our happiness, then we should either change it or leave it because the Lord has meant us to be happy, at least within the general limitations of our pilgrimage. But, if the problem is internal, as it is in most instances, then we are only kidding ourselves if we try to place the blame on others.

The one thing that we don't need more of is the neurotic, hate-filled, "liberal" preachers of the gospel of liberalism who have all the narrowness, rigidity and gloom of the most authoritarian conservative. Yet the gloomy "liberal," sober, solemn, serious, "revolutionary"—lay or clerical—seems to dominate the American scene. If one tells a joke at a meeting of "revolutionary" laity or at a clergy conference, he is greeted with the same pained silent indictment of tastelessness that one would expect if one blundered into a bedroom without knocking.

The Church needs visionaries of renewal. It needs joyous, happy and stouthearted men who realize that however desperate the situation is, it should never be permitted to get serious; and that while the lights in Camelot may go out, they always come back on again.

If most priests are not this kind of men, then I would submit that Catholicism is in a very bad way. If leadership does not come from men who laugh, it will come from men who hate. Most solemn, serious unlaughing men are haters if they have worked up enough energy to commit themselves to anything. And haters, no matter how great their enthusiasm, end up by destroying. Adolph Hitler and Joseph Stalin took themselves and their tasks very seriously. They rarely laughed, and they were quite incapable of any kind of play. But the wit of Churchill, de Gaulle, Roncalli and the Kennedy clan have already become part of the 20th century legend. Just as men who are expressive have far more influence over their fellows than men who merely administer, so do men who laugh and know how to play appeal far more powerfully to their fellows than those whose facial muscles quickly become sore as soon as the first lines of a smile begin to form.

There are a number of obstacles to hilarity. One is our Calvinistic, anti-Camelot work ethic which we have absorbed both from our seminary training and from American society. Far too many priests feel absolutely guilty if they are not on the move "doing something" every hour of their waking day. They report that they "have no time" to read, or to relax or to play. They may take their annual vacations; but they grow restless with the forced "inactivity" of the vacation, and they eagerly scan the death notices in the morning papers for a pretext to return to the city. They are also wary of other interests besides those that are immediately connected with their ministry, partly because of feelings of psychological inadequacy and partly because of the anti-intellectualism of the Catholic immigrant past. We have no time for art or music or opera, and only effeminate people are interested in that sort of thing.

It takes, I suppose, a great deal of personal security to

permit oneself to be enthusiastic about a number of different things. Yet it's paradoxically true that if we commit ourselves to a number of things, we are likely to do them all better than if we timidly focus on only one activity. The men of Camelot were multipurpose, Renaissance men who strove to do many different things well; the people who try to destroy Camelot are narrow, fixated men with a single idea who do all things badly.

Some of the most appalling experiences of my life have been at clerical gatherings, whether they be Forty-hour services, Confirmations, anniversary dinners or the installation of members of the hierarchy. I leave to others to agonize over the expense of such events. What disturbs me is their insufferable dullness. The talks are windy and not very clear; the conversations are stereotyped; the humor archaic, the good fellowship patently phony, and the joyousness distorted to the point of caricature. Camelot, indeed!

The virtues that we have described thus far are all linked intimately with one another. It is hard to be hilarious if we do not respect ourselves or enjoy the friendship of others. And we will not respect ourselves or others unless we are closely in touch with the nonrational elements of our life and able to give ourselves over to merriment. If we are really serious about wanting to create the future, then we must be playful. If we are not going to be playful, then we might as well give up hope in the future and content ourselves in living somberly in the past and practicing custody of the eyes in the process.

The good red wine is still around in American Catholicism though some of the sober, serious laity wonder if it ought not to be sold and the money given to the poor. But the laughter has not been heard for a long time. As one sober, serious layman said to a friend of mine, "There's just not much to laugh about."

[7]

Integrity

All organizations made up of human beings have a considerable amount of corruption within them, and the Catholic Church is no exception. Anyone who denies this fact knows nothing of Church history, ancient or modern. Surely one's faith in Christianity and the Church ought not to be grounded in the moral rectitude of its leadership. Whether the Church is more corrupt or less corrupt than other human organizations would be very difficult to judge, although the Church probably has less corruption in it now than it has had in most other times in its history. And much of the corruption currently existing in the Church is not the result of malice or lust as it often was in the past, but rather of ignorance and stupidity, and occasionally ambition. Although nepotism is no less a problem when the favorites who are promoted are not physical relatives, ability is probably less an obstacle to promotion within the Church than it has been at many times in the past.

It is not, however, my intention in this chapter to discuss the problems of the Church Universal and the high levels of ecclesiastical government. Instead, I will discuss the corruption that threatens us even at the very low levels of the priesthood. If we are to create the future, we must attain far more integrity than we have at the present time. By integrity I do not mean rigid, inflexible, doctrinaire "honesty" which forbids both urbanity and diplomacy and absolutely abhors compromise. By integrity I mean the opposite of that peculiar combination of mediocrity, paternalism, amateurism and lack of principle which characterizes much priestly behavior in many Catholic institutions and produces an utterly demoralizing effect on members of the institutions.

In the modern world decisions are, at least ideally, made on the basis of universalistic criteria. The efficency of modern society depends on men being promoted, at least to a considerable extent, on the basis of demonstrated competencies and skills because it is assumed that the health of society requires the best possible man be assigned to every position that is open. Admittedly, the principle of universalism is not always followed in practice, partly because favoritism survives, partly because there is always some doubt as to who the best man for a job is, and partly because in case of doubt we tend to choose those we like. But there are few organizations that are as bad as the Church when it comes to promoting men, not for what they know or what they can do but for what clique of friends they belong to and who they know. One has the awesome feeling that long after "clout" is eliminated from political life it will still be the common currency of ecclesiastical politics. One may well wonder whether American Catholisism is really going to be able to master its present challenges without developing a "civil service" for its bureaucrats and a method of electing its top leadership for limited terms of office.

As a result of our highly individualistic and particularistic method of assigning people to positions, we often find that critical positions from the pastor on up are manned by people who are totally unqualified for the job and yet who are tolerated and even protected because of obedience and respect. There is no point in not being bluntly honest about it. Drunks, homosexuals, womanizers, titanic bunglers and out and out madmen have held responsible positions far longer than they ought because in the name of virtue and piety those around them have covered their defects and surrounded them with reverence and awe. Their associates usually say that it is their obligation to protect the essential role of authority in the Church.

The possibility of covering up incompetency has declined; people in the parish no longer blind themselves and say that the pastor was sick again this morning. They now say bluntly, "The old man was drunk again." And the financial mismanagement of dioceses and archdioceses very quickly gets into the newspapers. Priests who run off with other men's wives announce the news of these happy events from the pulpit instead of sneaking off in silence and having their fellow clerics cover for them by saying that they are away on "sick leave." Nevertheless, we go on pretending, hiding the mediocrity and the incompetency on the grounds that the lay people would be scandalized if they knew. In truth they know all too well and are laughing at our pretense.

Let me emphasize that I am not saying that all leaders, or a majority or even a substantial minority are incompetent. But some are, and our refusal as individuals and as a collegium of clergy to face the moral implications of this incompetency has had a progressive corrupting influence on all of us.

We also seem to be incurable amateurs. The higher educational institutions have given up the polite fiction that anyone who graduated from a seminary can teach theology, but the feeling still seems to be widespread among the priesthood that almost anyone can do anything without the credentials required for the work or without adhering to the standards which others who do the same work must live by. If a religious superior decides that a man is to be a social work administrator, an educator, a press relations specialist, a director of research or an ecumenist, it is assumed that religious obedience makes the man qualified in this field, and nothing more is required. Indeed, if a man has had professional training in the area in question, he may well be considered too big a risk for the job because his professional competency and knowledge might make him "unsafe." So we turn most of our responsible positions over to canon lawyers because canon lawyers have generally been considered the safest of men.

We also try to be very familial in our relationships. We substitute an informal casual style for properly professional behavior and mix the pastoral touch in the midst of professional relationships whenever we can so that we may temper the rationality of a painful administrative decision with the reassurance that we are, after all, a "nice guy." One lay Catholic administrator told me about a meeting between himself, a university president and a faculty member who had been something less than careful in the exercise of his professional responsibilities. At the beginning of the conversation the faculty member asked the president, who was a priest, to bless a rosary for his wife. As the dean later put it to me, "That was the end. As soon as he pulled out the rosary and set up the relationship as a married man to a priest, I knew we had lost the case."

While we are casual and familial in our attempts to be pastoral, we are also paternalistic. Daddy, after all, knows best. He will trust his subordinates up to a point, but after that point he will take the matter out of the subordinates' hands, and in his supreme wisdom he will make the decision by himself. The corruption comes not so much in the paternalism, but by the subordinates' persistent refusal to resist the paternalism and by their acceptance of it without any complaints to "Big Daddy," but with many complaints to anybody else who will listen.

Finally, there is a great deal of dishonesty in the priestly brotherhood and some of the most appalling, craven flattering that anyone can find anywhere this side of Peking. Several times in my life I have been in the company of members of the hierarchy who have surrounded themselves with sychophants, men who are quite inept at anything but flattering the generally physically failing "old man." These have been horrendous experiences. While I am not inclined to drink, the temptation to wash the foul taste out of my mouth with a fairly large number of glasses of whisky and water was strong indeed. We flatter the incompetent, pretend that they are right, attempt to protect them from their mistakes, sacrifice others to them, complain behind their backs and compromise far beyond the point any sense of integrity allows. We defend ourselves from such inexcusable behavior and then wonder why we become corrupt and surround ourselves with lay people who are classic examples of demoralized corruption.

I know of one young lay person who was working in a Catholic administrative office and resigned in disgust when she could no longer tolerate the systematic corruption which existed in the level above her own administrative unit. She was astonished on the day when she walked out of the office because all the other lay people on the staff congratulated her and said that they wished they had the courage to do what she had done. The priests who were her superiors were good men, but they were caught in a situation where the very highest level in their own particular segment of the People of God was occupied by a corrupt and incompetent man. Their training and their practice inclined them to temporize, compromise, to tolerate, to excuse, plead and hope for their leader's demise. Unfortunately, they did not realize that they were becoming corrupt in the process, and they were spreading their own corruption to the lay people around them.

The border line between compromise and corruption is a thin one, and in any pattern of human relationships we must accept some things we don't like, and we must sacrifice some goods we would like to pursue in view of a larger common good. Nonetheless, there are some things that can't be compromised. There are some kinds of temporizing behavior that must be attributed not to prudence or discretion or diplomacy, but to fear and craven abdication of responsibility. In my own life as a priest I have on many occasions compromised far more than I ought to have and thus permitted myself to become corrupt. For example, in an attempt to keep alive a teen-age organization perennially threatened by Mother Superiors, janitors and presidents of altar societies, I tolerated the imposition on the teen-age club of restraints and restrictions that violated human dignity. In my anxiety to placate my superior I often treated some of these young people with much less dignity and respect than they were entitled to and which they certainty had every reason to demand from their priest.

It was so very easy to do, and of course it was what I was precisely trained to do—yield every other virtue to the demands of obedience and pretend that somehow or other my corruption would seem virtuous in the eyes of God. I suppose that if circumstances had not snatched me out of the institutional Church and into the secular university, I not only would have grown more corrupt, but would not even have realized the immorality of my corruption. I would surely not want to assert that corruption is not to be found in the world of the university, or the foundation or the federal government. It does exist, and in some ways it is as bad and even worse than the corruption found in the Church. It does seem to me, however, that the secular world has been more effective than the Church at minimizing corruption precisely because competence, professionalism, universalistic norms and some kinds of honesty have placed a premium on integrity. This attitude does not seem to exist in the Church.

Ecclesiastical leadership and, to some extent all priests, are shielded from hearing exactly what people think of them. If they were not so shielded, they would be far more concerned about integrity than they are now. They would be far more aware that large numbers of Catholic people neither believe nor trust their ecclesiastical leadership. If we are to create the future, we must do our best to curtail the corruption which exists in the Church, to expose it at every level in the ecclesiastical organization and demand that it end. Just as Paul demanded that Peter end a compromise which he thought threatened to corrupt the early Church, we must curtail corruption.

We must try to eliminate corruption because it severely limits our credibility with our people and demoralizes our spirit. It is impossible to expect ourselves to trust others, to be playful, hopeful and sensitive to the world when we are aware in our heart of hearts that much of our behavior is false, and that we are hiding incompetency, stupidity, and on occasion dishonesty, behind a smooth, bland, clerical smile.

This has been a blunt chapter and many priests will argue that it is scandalous to say these sorts of things in public print, but it would be an even greater scandal to pretend that corruption is not a problem, especially when the overwhelming majority of laity are only too well aware of the problem and are growing tired pretending out of reverence that it really isn't there.

[8]

Tolerance

Tolerance is a virtue that has been receiving some fairly rough treatment in the modern world. Just as the Catholic Church gets around, finally, to officially approving religious toleration (an idea which, of course, was rooted in the Gospel message that the Church has preached for 2,000 years) some of the liberal left, led by Professor Herbert Marcuse, have begun to affirm that too much tolerance may be a bad thing and that those things which are "wrong" should not be tolerated. This notion sounds too much like the old ecclesiastical dictum that error had no rights. On the other hand, many young people who are not willing to go along with the student extremists who are disciples of Professor Marcuse will nonetheless argue that the extremists, white and black, must be permitted to do "their thing," no matter what it is. It must be confessed that both positions are quite lacking in appeal.

I would define tolerance as the capacity for suspending judgment, keeping balance, and asking questions without demanding immediate answers. The wise man, the man who wants to create the future, strives to blend tolerance for the new or the different with skepticism about it.

Skepticism is a somewhat short commodity in contemporary Catholicism. The structure of many of our old certainties has produced a situation in which new fads and fashions abound. The ebb and flow of fads and fashions is aggravated by the fact that we are attempting to wrestle with critical and complex intellectual problems with a very small group of trained and disciplined scholars, many of whom, particularly if they are theologians, are worked to death by the constant demands made on their time and talent for lectures, articles and advice.

The need for skepticism was made forcefully clear to me at a recent meeting of Protestants and Catholics in discussing the future of the ministry. On the whole, I think the Catholic priests attending the meeting were brighter, more insightful and more enthusiastic than their Protestant counterparts, but they were also intellectually undisciplined to an embarrassing extent. They were committed to one-shot, simplified answers, and engaged in the repetition of cliches and undefined catch words—the favorites are still "community" and "structure." Their conversation was totally innocent of nuance and shading. They seemed to perceive the world as composed of blacks or whites and approached it in a style of either/or.

I was somewhat embarrassed after a number of these priests engaged in lengthy and confused outbursts in which passion and "sincerity" were clearly intended to substitute for articulation and cogency. My embarrassment increased when a Protestant would calmly and coolly take them apart by the simple process of agreeing with everything they said, and then affirming that "on the other hand" a lot could be said for exactly the opposition position, too. What was most disturbing was that my Catholic conferees did not realize that the Protestant speaker was not agreeing with them. Politely, but firmly, he was cutting them into ribbons.

A Catholic bishop who is also a distinguished scholar commented to me later on, "What our men lack is a sense of method." By this he meant that they did not seem to realize that in the world of scholarship in which they were moving, conclusions based on insight are not offered for consideration until the insight has been documented by a slow, careful collection of evidence, the weighing of contrary possibility and the development of a balanced and carefully-worded presentation of what the scholar wants to say. While some of our enthusiasts are quite enamored of such scholars as Hans Kung and Karl Rahner, they do not display their sense of "method" as they try to push their theological conclusions into practical programs.

It has occurred to me while pondering this phenomenon of the enthusiast that in some respects these men represent the opposite side of the coin that we normally think of as being the image of the intransigent conservative. Both have a definite need for certainty as a result of inadequate intellectual training which insisted on perceiving the world as black and white, either or, and taught them to think analytically rather than synthetically. We should not, therefore, be surprised that yesterday's radical innovators become today's stunted conservatives. The old radicals turned to new conservatives have not changed, nor have their ideas or their intellectual style changed. But the world has changed, and they can't. If you scratch a twenty-seven year old radical priest, you'll find a forty-five year old reactionary. The family movements, labor schools, Gregorian chant, inquiry classes, juvenile delinquency, marriage counseling and even the missal represent the liberal certainties of the past, just as the inner city, picketing, sensitivity training, postcard surveys, concelebration, Mass without vestments and dialogue homilies represent the liberal certainties of the present.

Furthermore, we are faced with the rise and decline of the prophets. In the late 1940's it was Thomas Merton. In the early 1950's it was Jean Danielou and Yves Congar. In the late 1950's and early 1960's it was Bernard Haring and Karl Rahner. More recently there have been Hans Kung, Edward Schillebeeckx and John McKenzie. At the present time the hottest names are Leslie Dewart, Paul Van Buren and Harvey Cox. These various prophets who have appeared on the scene are quoted with the same awe and frequently the same lack of understanding as the old style Dominicans (of the 1940's and 1950's) used to quote St. Thomas Aquinas. All this, of course, is very much a substitute for thought. Unless we are capable of thinking critically, we will not be strong enough or flexible enough to create the future.

The tolerant man does not reject the past because it is past or enthuse over the new because it is new. He does not write off the family movement or youth work as being worthless because they were done ten or fifteen years ago, nor is he convinced that the "T" group is universally applicable to every conceivable situation simply because it is new, or at least newly discovered in the Church. Nor does he think that it is unnecessary to read Danielou because Leslie Dewart provides all the answers. Nor would he, as one liberal sociologist has done, automatically score a respondent as conservative because the respondent happened to read one of Father Leen's books. The tolerant man and the skeptical man are really the same man. Both possess the open mind. They have strength to keep their minds open despite the pressure towards closure on the subject of the past and on the subject of the present. On the other hand, the tyrannical pastor and the doctrinaire curate are brothers under the skin because both have closed minds. The man of tolerance is the man who is able to be skeptical even about himself. Incidentally, this is no mean feat.

It seems to me that the secret of tolerance and skepticism is to be able to see the adversary's point of view, to understand it in its historical, cultural and social context, to be able to listen to it, to try to integrate its insights, into our own vision and to listen carefully to its implications for our own behavior. We are able to do this, of course, if our own position is clearly thought out, precisely articulated and open-ended. But if our position is closed; if we have a strong need for dogmatic certainty, then we cannot listen, we cannot understand and we cannot combine. We forget that dogmatic certainty is always a disguise for uncertainty.

One of the more striking phenomena of the post-conciliar Church has been our ability to dialogue with our separated brother, and our serious lack of ability to dialogue with ourselves. The separated brother apparently is excused for disagreeing with us because his historical and cultural experience is presumed to have left him in good faith. But those who are a part of the same household of faith as we ought to know better than to disagree with us. Hence, they are presumed to be in bad faith, malicious or incompetent. We have done a neat flip-flop. Not so long ago we denounced other religious leaders and passionately defended our own. Now we are most sympathetic to the religious leaders of others and passionately denounce our own. There is, one supposes, some progress in this flip-flop, but not much.

There seem to be a number of reasons for our rigidity, narrowness and intolerance. Perhaps most basic is the personal insecurity of our own lives. A man who is uncertain about his own selfhood disguises his own uncertanty by passionate and unnegotiable affirmations about everything else that crosses his range of vision. Secondly, our training was dogmatic in the extreme. Those who were alleged to disagree with us were set up as "straw men" and then cut to ribbons with our sophisticated arsenal of Scripture text, syllogisms, references to the Fathers and conciliar arguments. In three or four pages of the philosophy manual we proved Kant "wrong", but we never bothered to understand what he was trying to do, what valuable insights he offered, or why he has had such a profound and pervasive influence on the modern world. In addition, most of those of us who had intellectual talent were not given the opportunity to refine, develop and broaden this talent in graduate school training. In the absence of the discipline of such professional training, our insight and our intuitions, however rich, were not sharpened, focused, ordered or reinforced. As a result our intellectual equipment is a bit out of kilter, a bit incomplete and occasionally somewhat deformed. I am certainly not asserting that graduate school training is absolutely essential for intellectual discipline or certainly produces it. There are many priests with finely disciplined minds who have never set foot inside a university, and many sadly deformed ones have been on university campuses for long periods of time. But graduate school training is extremely useful to the man with an acute intellect.

Finally, there is the extension of the "style of infallibility" in vast areas of ecclesiastical administration and decision-making where it has no right to be. Papal infallibility is a strictly defined and rarely used charism, but personal infallibility seems to be a charism that a vast multiude of office holders in the Church, some of them extremely unimportant, take almost as a matter of course. We need only look around to note all too many men in responsible positions who are often in error but never in doubt. Before long we find ourselves imitating them.

The tolerant open mind is not common in the priesthood either among the old or the young. Perhaps because of my advancing years I find intolerance even more insufferable in the young than in the old because in the young intolerance parades under the name of liberalism. Yet two relatively simple considerations ought to make us very suspicious of magic answers, the magic answers of the past or those of the present. First of all, no previous magic answer in history has worked. The Church has consistently made progress, but there isn't much reason, if one looks at the historical evidence, to assume that sensitivity training or marching on picket lines is going to advance our progress towards the Omega point any more rapidly than did reading the missal, active participation in the liturgy or the Sorrowful Mother Novena. This is not to argue that picketing or "T" groups are wrong or ineffective, but merely to say that the historical evidence suggests that any innovation is likely to have at best limited effectiveness. It does not mean we should not innovate, but it means that we should not have too high expectations about what will come from innovations.

Secondly, as I have suggested in a book called *The Crucible of Change*,* what we know of the structure of human society and of the human personality leads us to believe that religious progress will necessarily be slow because of massive resistance by individuals and by society. A legendary Chicago alderman is alleged to have argued that "Chicago isn't ready for reform yet." Neither is the human race quite ready for Christianity yet, even if Christianity were to be presented in a most attractive and sophisticated form. No matter how much we improve our techniques, the massive indifference and apathy of mankind is not likely to give way, at least not in the present state of developments.

The counsel of realism is not the counsel of despair. Our progress will necessarily be slow, but we are not excused from innovation. On the contrary, the obligation to innovation is stronger when we recognize that progress must be slow. If one innovation won't solve our problem,

* New York: Sheed & Ward, 1968.

then clearly we need many innovations. But tolerance, and on its reverse side, skepticism, are not virtues which turn us into conservatives. They ought to convert us into sensible and sensitive men who are neither afraid to innovate nor compelled to accept every proposed innovation that appears. As creators of the future, we certainly must innovate. But we should not waste our time, energy or concern on innovations that are proposed by crackpots and documented only by personal opinion.

Tolerance is, I think, closely related to hilarity. Most reformers who are obsessed with single-shot, simple-minded answers are notoriously unhumorous. They can't afford to be humorous, of course, because if you have the answer to everyone's problems you would be derelict in your duty if you didn't spend every second of your time pushing that answer. If you had the perspective and the sensitivity to be able to laugh at yourself, you'd understand how utterly absurd it is to think that your ideas are going to work wonders when everyone else's have failed. The very absence of laughter and humor in much of the current "reform" agitation in contemporary Catholicism gives us some idea of how many intolerant and unskeptical men there are abroad in the land.

Nor does one generation of radicals learn from the lessons of the previous generation. Just as the picketing members of the new breed laugh at the family movement liberals of the generation before them, so inevitably there will arise a generation of clergy who find that those who are fixated on the problems of the inner city are politically naive and irrelevant because they don't understand where the action really is. If Harvey Cox is any predictor of the future the action will be in suburbia. The young would be very sophisticated indeed if they realized that someday they will be replaced by a newer generation of radicals who will reject them just as surely as they rejected their elders.

There are two ways to avoid this built-in, ecclesiastical obsolescence. The first way is to be a floater, that is, to keep one's convictions flexible and fluid enough so that they can change on a minute's notice and keep in very close touch with those sources which will give the first hint of changing fashions. The clerical floater who started out with the YCS and then progressed from the family movements to liturgical participation, racial justice, sensitivity training, and finally to student radicalism has done more than come the full circle. He has demonstrated agility in keeping up with fashions which might in other circumstances serve him in good stead as the editor of the woman's page of a daily newspaper. It's really not so difficult to do. All that is required is that one scan the pages of *The Christian Century*, *The National Catholic Reporter*, *The Commonweal* and *New Republic* carefully each week. A reader who follows these journals the way a fashionable woman reads *Vogue* or *Harper's Bazaar* has reasonable confidence that he will stay in fashion even though a new arbiter of fashion may come on the scene without warning.

The other way of avoiding clerical obsolescence is to develop the habit of asking for evidence from others and from one's self, of systematically reevaluating one's own convictions and methods while at the same time taking a good hard look at other people's bright and brave new ideas. To some extent our ability to engage in these activities depends upon our personality. Some of us tend to be a bit more hardnosed than others, but the creator of the future must be enthusiastic. However, he'd better not be an enthusiast. If he is, he runs the serious risk of becoming fixated either in the past or in the present which quickly becomes the past.

Some argue that the proper style for a cleric is to be neither the first nor the last to try something new. This is a coward's advice. Sometimes our circumstances and experience may demand that we be the first. At other times we must be true enough to ourselves and our insights to run the risk of being the last. I, for one, will certainly be the very last person to make a Cursillo. The tolerant man, the skeptical man does not fall victim to cliches, catchwords or slogans. And "neither the first nor the last" is just one more slogan masquerading as wisdom. As the creators of the future, we must cope with uncertainty and complexity. The temptation to find quick, cheap certainties is strong. Tolerance isn't easy, but then it wasn't intended to be.

[9]
Piety

We are witnessing a mammoth withdrawal of consensus within the Catholic Church. People are not leaving the Church in large numbers or even in small numbers substantial enough to show up in national surveys, but the clergy and the laity alike seem to be denying the right of ecclesiastical authority to impose binding obligations.

If we are to believe the Catholic press, Pope Paul was five times persuaded either by progressives or conservatives to put off issuing his encyclical on birth control, and we fear that at this stage of the game the Pope's eventual decision made little difference.

An overwhelming number of married Catholics had long since made their own decisions about birth control, and large numbers of priests had made their own decisions, too. I want to make it perfectly clear that I'm giving an objective description and not a defense of either side in the controversies I am discussing in this chapter. The Breviary, which was once considered to be such a solemn obligation by American priests that they were quite capable of pulling a car over to the side of the highway at a quarter to twelve and finishing None, Vespers and Compline by flashlight, is rapidly falling into disuse. The joke about the newly ordained priests in the seminary trying to sell their breviaries to the new subdeacons who refuse to buy them has become decidedly old hat. Underground parishes are emerging around the country without canonical status and their members are engaging in liturgical experimentations which far exceed the bounds of present regulations, and, on occasion, also of good taste. Many Catholic young people no longer consider themselves bound by the Sunday Mass obligation though they cheerfully go to Mass during the week instead. Not only parish priests, but even some marriage court officials give advice on the marriage legislation of the Church which is completely at variance with such legislation: "You know that the first marriage was invalid, and I know the first marriage is invalid. But we'll never get a decision through ecclesiastical courts in the present legislation, so you should exchange marriage vows, receive the sacraments and forget about the whole matter." The regulations about precensorship of books have become a joke to lay people writing in theological and religious areas, and have decreasing importance even among clergy and religious. Public statements of those in authority are not merely ignored. They are frequently derided.

This withdrawal of consensus is still selective and pertains to areas viewed as canonical and merely human regulation which do not have any relationship with the core of Catholic faith. When conservatives respond that the birth control matter does pertain to the core of faith, they are usually greeted with cynical laughter. Although the withdrawal of the consensus is selective, it is very widespread and may very well indicate a complete collapse of governance and law in the Church. There are a number of reasons for this withdrawal of consensus. First of all, it's perfectly clear that many laws and structures within the Church are obsolete and hurt rather than help the Church. There is widespread agreement that the marriage legislation needs drastic reform, but the reform does not take place. Although Catholics can be confident that it will take place, those who are faced with immediate problems see no reason why human lives should be messed up by marriage legislation when such legislation is obviously going to be changed anyhow.

Second, there is in many instances a complete failure on the part of the leadership to understand the complexity of the problems. I have the impression that liturgical reform usually comes about a year too late. Many moderates have already insituted on their own a reform by the time authority gets around to deciding that the reform is necessary. Those engaged in campus ministry, for example, are painfully aware of how desperately they need experimental liturgy if they're going to respond to the religious needs of college students. After repeated attempts they have not been able to make this need clear to those in leadership, or the leadership does not seem to be able to make the need clear to the Sacred Congregation of Rites. Those on the campus ministry then argue that the religious need of their people and of the Church is more important than juridical legislation and that the legislation ought to be ignored. Authority frequently responds by condemning the disobedience, but does not seem to understand the roots of the situation which caused the disobedience.

Third, the suddenness of the ideological and structural change within the church has released the pent-up frustrations of decades. When men and women felt that no change was possible they could grit their teeth and put up with what they thought was stupidity on the grounds that it was God's will. But now that change is possible, and yet is slow in coming, the bitterness erupts in anger and contempt for authority. The suddenness and the violence with which the Catholic laity have wrenched away consent on sexual matters from ecclesiastical authority is in part rooted in the belief that the whole birth control issue had been badly bungled during the past two decades.

Finally, many priests and religious have been trained systematically to be naive and immature, and many laity, otherwise sophisticated, are quite naive and immature in matters religious. Such lack of sophistication might have been functional for the organizational unity of the Church in a time of stability, but in a time of transition it simply aggravates and reinforces the problems.

There can be no doubt that the revolt against canonical authority permits meeting human needs which would otherwise not be met. Free Church liturgy, the underground parish, "unofficial" new marriage legislation and the anticipation of a change in birth control interpretation have removed burdens, which were severe and perhaps even intolerable, from the lives of many people. It is "easier" to be a Catholic now than it used to be, and so people are more likely to stay in the Church than to leave it. Renewal is being forced by this withdrawal of consensus. There is a "cultural lag" between the theories of Vatican II and the present structure of the Church. The theory calls for communication between the people and its leadership and for a responsiveness from the leadership to the people. But there is little communication taking place and precious little responsiveness. So change in the structures will take place probably only through the pressure of extralegal organizations of priests and lay people. One of the major challenges the ecclesiastical leadership faces is not to suppress these organizations, because they cannot be suppressed, but to involve them in the legal process of Church activity. However, "legal" may mean something very different today than it did to the collators of the Code of Canon Law. Pressures from the outside do speed up the pace of change in the church just as they do in all human organizations.

The withdrawal of consensus has also led to a more relaxed attitude toward law in the American Church. Common in most European countries, including Italy, this attitude never did become part of American Catholicism. Perhaps the new Church in the new world wanted to be more Roman than the pope. A European priest would think that an American cleric pulled over on the side of the highway reading the breviary by flashlight was uproariously funny.

Finally, the current spirit of disregard for the law may force churchmen to realize that law and institutions exist to serve human beings and not vice versa. I suspect that the immense success of James Kavanaugh's book* in part represents the bitter resentment of many Catholics for what seems to them harsh and arbitrary decisions made by the clergy in the name of Canon Law. The pastors who systematically refused to permit priest friends to officiate at marriages, funerals or Baptisms on the grounds that they alone had the right to officiate at such ceremonies did uphold their own legal rights, but they offended countless thousands of people by doing so. At times they aggravated situations where there was already great family emotion. As we pay the penalty for the decisions of these harsh and rigid men, we may begin to understand that law is not an end in itself.

There are very considerable disadvantages in the withdrawal of consensus we are witnessing. Once authority loses its credibility or throws it away, there is nothing to prevent the emergence of a lunatic fringe and its seizure of power and prestige. We hear of the liturgy being celebrated with Coca-Cola and hotdog buns on the grounds that this is the bread and wine of teen-agers, or with Rye-Crisp and martinis because this is the bread and wine of the suburban set. Some of those who have set up their own laws on birth control and on marriage have also proclaimed that premarital sexuality, extra marital sexuality and even homosexuality are, after all, quite in keeping with Christian virtue. When group discussions become prayer and the only kind of prayer that is needed, everybody becomes a priest; the most absurd and insane amateur

* *A Modern Priest Looks at His Outdated Church* (New York: Trident Press, 1967).

theological meanderings become a new orthodoxy, and the struggle to become more outlandish than anyone else becomes the top item on everyone's agenda.

At the root of the problem, however, is the collapse of order. By order I do not mean uniformity; I do not mean rigid military discipline; and I do not mean inflexibility which does not permit experiment. I mean that kind of unity without which it is impossible for a community or a people to survive as a meaningful social unit. It is reasonable to assume that everyone is not an expert on everything. Nor is everyone qualified to be a completely adequate judge in his own case. Nor is everyone capable of judging with precision and accuracy what is the best for the whole Church and for every other individual Christian. The unity I have in mind ought to be based on respect for responsible scholarship, a sound interpretation of doctrinal tradition, good taste and mutual help and cooperation. As one reads through the Gospels and the Epistles, one can't help but conclude that the Lord intended that there be some such unity in his church. The Apostles were the men responsible for creating this unity and they took their responsibilities very seriously. It seems to me that it is precisely this kind of unity which is being seriously threatened by the current withdrawal of consensus.

I really don't pretend to know how the problem is going to be solved. It's bad, and it will probably get worse before it begins to get better. The polarization between authority that does not understand the problem and extremist elements who want no unity in the Church at all, is likely to continue, much to the confusion and discomfort of the vast, moderate majority caught in between. I am inclined to think that the problem will be solved only when we're able to clarify our notions of what authority is.

In the old view a person in authority was a person who had all the answers. He had been given the responsibility for providing the right answers, a responsibility which it would have been immoral for him to delegate. It was his task to do the thinking, the deciding and then to compel agreement. It is assumed that in such circumstances the one possessing authority had a near monopoly on wisdom and on access to the Holy Spirit. There wasn't much for him to learn, nor much for him to forget; the problems were fixed, and so were the answers in every last detail.

A newer view is that the Church has no power at all. It's only authority is one of love and service. Therefore, there should be no laws, no institutions, no patterns of behavior, only a community of love rather like one of the hippie communities in the Big Sur country. It is argued that if the Church has organizational patterns and regulations it is no different from any other human organization and cannot be "assigned to the nations."

Now it seems to me that the basic weakness of the new view is that it assumes the same description of authority as does the old view. It takes for granted the notion that authority must necessarily be repressive, dogmatic, authoritarian and probably self-seeking. The old view says that the Church must have authority; the new view says that the Church must not have authority. Both agree that authority is something either feudal or Renaissance. The reader who finds this debate vaguely familiar would be quite correct

in his suspicion. It is the old debate between Thomas
Hobbes and Jean Jacques Rousseau, interesting historically,
but irrelevant to the problems of the modern world. It
would be helpful if the present debaters on authority in the
Church realized that there have been theorizers about the
nature of authority since Hobbes and Rousseau, for example, John Locke, Thomas Jefferson, John Kenneth Gal-
braith and Peter Drucker. Those blithe young enthusiasts
who insist that authority in the Church is "different" because it is "an authority of service" would be well advised
to read the Constitution of the United States or any text-
book on personnel management. In the modern world all
authority claims to be and in many instances actually is an
authority of service. Secondly, those partisans of either the
old or the new view who think that authority is necessarily
repressive and monarchical would be well advised to read
The Federalist Papers.

A third view is in keeping with the mainstream of the
Western political tradition which probably represents the
noblest concept of the nature of governance and authority
that men have ever developed. The present debaters over
authority in the Church should study the Western democratic tradition.

This tradition argues that authority exists to protect the
rights and the freedom of the individual citizen and to promote the general welfare of the society. Authority exists
to create a situation of relative stability and order because
human communities require a minimum of stability and
order in the relationship patterns among the members of
the community. By the way, for the nonsociologists, who

insistently use the term "structure," this stability in relationship patterns is what structure really is.

Authority is responsible for the bookkeeping and housekeeping details of the community. But as we've suggested in an earlier chapter, the primary purpose of authority is to influence the minds and hearts of the people in the community, principally by asking the critical questions that are relevant to the purposes for which communities exist. Authority sees the vision of the common good and prods the members of the community to take their minds and their concerns off their individual goods long enough to see the implications of the common good and to strive for its fulfillment. Authority presides over a consensus. It is able to attain consensus not merely, or not even primarily by commanding, but rather by promoting communication between itself and the rest of the community and among the various groups within the community. To achieve consensus and communication authority attempts to facilitate maximum participation in the decision making of the community. It's goal is to obtain the best possible information and insight in the making of decisions and to guarantee the maximum possible cooperation in the implementation of the decision. Finally, authority directs and supervises the execution of the community decisions.

In this view of authority the function of leadership is not primarily either coercive or permissive, although both coerciveness and permissiveness are part of its role. Its function is to stimulate, encourage, protect, promote, consult, coordinate and collaborate. Anyone wishing further details on this Western tradition of authority and governments might consult, as I've suggested before, *The Federalist Papers* or the encyclicals *Quadragesimo Anno* and *Pacem in Terris*.

Any human community needs authority and governance of the sort that I've described as being envisaged by the Western political tradition. Such authority is particularly imperative in the complicated, corporate society in which we live. It is required not because man is evil as Hobbes would say. Nor can we dispense with it because man is good as Rousseau would say. Authority is needed in the tradition of men like Locke, Jefferson and John XXIII because man is limited and can't think of everything at the same time.

All of these considerations may seem to have very little to do with the subject of "piety" which the title of this chapter seemed to indicate that we were going to discuss, but "piety" in the ancient Roman sense meant more than religious devotion. It meant fidelity and respect for authority even if, as in the case of Virgil's Aeneas, the authority's plans and wishes were something less than systematically codified. In spite of the widespread disrespect for authority demonstrated in the Church today, the Church, like all human communities, needs authority. However, authority should be exercised in a very different style from the way it is used today. Authority is not respected at the present time because the behavior of some of those in authority has led them to throw away respect and credibility, and because authority is failing to fulfill the principal function for which it exists.

Yet we will not create the future unless our efforts are

coordinated; unless we have a common tradition around which to rally; unless we have leaders who force us to consider the common good and who challenge us to refresh our vision and rethink our activities. Therefore we must deeply respect the principle and the ideal of authority. Our principal concern must be to make that authority effective on all levels. When authority in the Church is effective, it need not worry about credibility or respect because both will be received automatically.

[10]

Enthusiasm

One evening not so long ago I was sitting in the living room of a house on the edge of a great city listening to a very painful attempt at communication between a group of very young priests and seminarians and a group of lay people their own age. It was a strange sort of meeting because the laity were acting very differently than the myth created by the liberal press would have us believe. They were highly incensed with the insistence of the clergy that priests could behave "like anyone else," and that there were no specific priestly activities beyond the liturgy that could be demanded of the clergy. The laity, on the other hand, were insisting, I thought somewhat fiercely, that priests were leaders and should act like leaders, and that since they were religious leaders they should act like religious human beings. It was, I think, a very painful experience for the young clergy because they had dedicated themselves to systematically destroying in their value system every trace of the old clerical culture. Now they were being told by a group of their contemporaries whose liberalism and dedication was beyond question that they had pushed the declericalization too far and now ought to start behaving like priests. For the laity, the problem was somewhat different. They knew what they wanted, but they didn't have the terminology to articulate it. They wanted their priests to be warm and humanly concerned about them, but they also wanted them to be *priests*.

Finally, one somewhat outspoken young woman got to the core of the problem. "How come," she demanded. "I never hear anything enthusiastic from you people? The Church is changing dramatically; there are all kinds of exciting things going on; we have opportunities that we haven't had for centuries, and I don't hear about any of these things from you. All of us in this room spent a lot of time working enthusiastically for the Church and for our fellowmen, and we don't see any of this from you. What's the matter with you guys?"

A deacon casually flicked the ashes off his cigarette and replied, "Don't you think it's rather absurd for you to expect the clergy to have more enthusiasm and dedication than you have?"

There were profanities and even obscenities uttered in response to that statement, but clearing the responses from their somewhat more colorful trappings, we could summarize them in these words, "We sure do expect it."

The priest who can do nothing more than relate to his people his own confusions, problems, and identity crisis and who spends most of his time lamenting the depraved structures of the Church or the massive obstacles to social change is hardly likely to be a creator of the future. Enthusiasm is not an optional quality in a priest. It is absolutely imperative if one is to lead other human beings, particularly young ones. The man who is unable to be enthusiastic about the mission of the Church or the vision of the Gospel doesn't belong in the priesthood and never did belong there.

I've been asked many times what quality I think is most important in working with young people despite the fact that my reputation as an expert on young people is based largely on a decade of failure. But it does seem to me that the absolutely indispensable quality for anyone who intends to work with young people is enthusiasm. You don't need to be an athlete, a guitar player, a folk singer, a comedian, or an extrovert to be good with kids. You do have to be enthusiastic because they are inclined to be enthusiastic themselves. But the adult society they see around them warns them that if they show any enthusiasm they are going to be jumped. So when an adult comes along and says to them that there are grounds for enthusiasm and for hope, the young person comes alive and listens eagerly to what this enthusiastic person has to say.

On the basis of a fair number of interviews I have the impression that most young priests do not want to work with young people. They argue that they are adult males, and they want to work with other adult males and not be tied down to the "kiddie apostolate." It seems to me that they're uncertain, not only about their masculinity, but also about their adulthood.

I think I can understand the problem. In my own days in the "kiddie apostolate" I found the business and professional men of the community to be quite insufferable in their assumption that "their" world, the world of business and profession, was the *real* world and that I was nothing more than a somewhat well-trained babysitter, a part of the world of women and children. ("You're really doing fine work with the kids, Father.") I was furious about being relegated to the role of second-rate male, and I retaliated by suggesting, none too urbanely, that they were the ones who were second-rate males and second-rate husbands and fathers to boot.

It didn't seem to me then, and it doesn't now, that we can legitimately assess our vision of what is real and what is unreal from what other people say. Having had experience since then in the world of the professions, I am prepared to make a fairly strong case that adolescent society is every bit as real, somewhat more adult and certainly more pleasant and more human. If I must choose between teen-agers and full professors as people with whom to play, I will take the teen-agers any day of the week and cheerfully concede the full professors to the tender care of the junior clergy.

More important than our own inclinations is the incontrovertible fact that the adolescent years are the ones when the work of the priest is likely to be most effective. The behavioral sciences tell us beyond all doubt that adolescence is the best time in life to modify the human personality. It is the time of a "second chance" when the mistakes and the injuries of the childhood years can be substantially corrected, and when the openness, the generosity, the enthusiasm of the human personality can be solidly rooted so that they will survive for the rest of the person's life. The young priests tell me that they are unable or unwilling to work with young people because the young people are not adults. I am forced to reply that these priests themselves are not adults because an adult is able to judge what is the most effective kind of work he can do, and because a mature adult is able to generate enthusiasm. Adult enthusiasm is not the shallow, fluid enthusiasm of the pursuer of fashions. It is the substantial hardnosed, mature enthusiasm of the committed, intelligent man of the world. The cynical, blasé younger clergy who cannot become enthusiastic about work with youth have become old and decrepit before their time exactly because they have resolutely refused to play the proper role of the young adult male to "see visions."

The younger clergy cannot become enthusiastic about adolescents, and many of the older clergy argue that enthusiasm is a waste of time. It does not work, they say. The kids will let you down; they'll break your heart; they'll never do what they say they'll do and will never be the kind of people you think they are going to be.

Well, maybe, but again, it depends on what sort of response one expects and demands. As I have suggested earlier, it is unrealistic to expect to have an impact on very many young people given the state of mankind and our knowledge of human behavior. The influence of family, peer group, community is not (Catholic Action moderators to the contrary) going to be changed by one YCS meeting or even for most people by years of intense interaction with any cleric. We really don't understand how you change or liberate the human personality, though we are beginning to. The Church, despite its current fascination with sensitivity training, is not paying much attention to what we do know on the subject. However, if our goals are not to change humanity as a mass, but to profoundly influence a few and to that extent also their children and their children's children; and if we thereby slowly push back the boundaries of hatred and fear and disgust in the world, then we can be reasonably confident of success in our work with young people. Our losses will be greater than our victories, but the victories we win will be big ones.

I also feel that we really don't understand what the young people expect of us or what shape they want our enthusiasm to take. In my decade of working with adolescents, I assumed that these intelligent, docile, talented, upper middle class Irish teen-agers required vision and motivation. It was my job to portray a vision of the possibilities of the Christian life and the human life in our time and then strongly motivate them to pursue this vision enthusiastically and vigorously despite the opposition, bourgeois culture in which they were enmeshed. I must confess that most of my enthusiasm was quite ineffective.* The young people listened politely, kept coming back and discussed in a very intelligent and sophisticated fashion the ideas I was propounding. They seemed to agree with me completely, but then they went off to college and in short order became every bit as bourgeois as their parents and older brothers and sisters. Depending upon the amount of sleep I had had on the previous night I blamed them for being unreceptive or myself for being unpersuasive.

It was only after I had left the parish and came to know many of these young people in a far different kind of relationship that I finally understood what the problem had

* For examples of my argumentation and motivation, see *And Young Men Shall See Visions* (New York: Sheed & Ward, 1964) and *Letters to Nancy* (New York: Sheed & Ward, 1964).

been. It was not that they did not understand me, or did not find the vision of the Church I offered attractive. They found it very attractive, indeed. But they didn't believe that it was a possible vision for them because they did not believe they were good enough for it.

What they needed from me was not prophecy or per-susasion. They needed reassurance that they were worth something, that they merited love and that their priest loved them. They wanted me to be enthusiastic about them as human beings. Of course, I was, but nothing in my training or experience enabled me to understand how important such enthusiasm was to them or how it might be communicated. Raised as so many of them had been in an atmosphere of conditioned love where they had to earn by success even the faintest praise, they needed to be told that there was something in their personalities which could move me to enthusiasm. I am afraid that I failed them.

Some priests are able to generate enthusiasm for projects and programs, for dances, or plays or visiting the sick or even marching in a picket line. But what young people really need is someone who is a visionary *for them;* they need someone who is enthusiastic *about them,* someone who can view them, not as members of an organization, but lonely, frightened, fragile, traumatized human beings who are going through the most critical years of their lives. If the right appeal is made by the right person at the right time the whole shape of their future can be changed.

The teen-ager responds to the man of enthusiasm be-cause he wants to believe that enthusiasm is possible. He wants to believe that cynicism, apathy, and indifference are not the necessary fates of his dreams and hopes. If a priest has an enthusiastic vision and a vision which the adolescent feels is *for him*, then his response is bound to be positive. There may be considerable difficulties in the relationship between the priest and the adolescent, but at least the enthusiastic priest has made a good beginning.

There is in every man a bit of the teen-ager, a bit of the fond hope that indifference, apathy and complacency are not necessarily the only available style of response to the challenges of life. Teen-agers may be the most receptive enthusiasts, but only the most hardened and stagnated of human beings is immune to enthusiasm. The man with vision, enthusiasm, restlessness, the willingness to take chances, the man who will not be discouraged, at least not permanently, the man who is ready to start all over again even though he knows he is going to face many of the same frustrations and pains that have already battered against him, this is the man other men will follow. The priest who is not capable of generating enthusiasm is the priest who has lost his nerve and quite possibly lost his faith, too.

I make no claim that enthusiasm is easy. It isn't easy when one is over thirty, and it's far less easy when one is over forty. I lay no claim to being without fault myself in sustaining enthusiasm. Last winter I received a phone call from a young lady whom I had taught in grammar school many years before. She and her classmates were now seniors in high school soon to be going off to college. They wondered if it would be possible to have a discussion group like the ones we used to have for high school seniors in days gone by. Unfortunately for her, she called just at the point that the Green Bay Packers were kicking off. I thought of all the frustrations of past teen-age groups, of all the suspicious, complaining parents, the tardy, unreliable adolescents, the endless discussions and the very minor impact of all the activity. Then I very unenthusiastically told the young lady that I would think about it and call her back. I settled down to watch the Packers chew up another team (the Chicago Bears), but the young lady's cousin looked down upon me from his picture on the wall with a stern, disapproving frown. I guess it does help to be related to a cardinal even if he's dead. So, I called her back immediately—well, almost immediately. I waited until half time.

The priest is supposed to be a prophet. Some of us are able to be good prophets because of the state of our digestive and circulatory systems. Others have the kind of personality that will keep us prophesying until we breathe our last breath; but most of us are prophets because of little more than internal convictions and hard work. We almost quit every week or so; scarcely a day passes when we're not discouraged. We are presumably the salt of the earth, and almost every morning of our lives we should ask ourselves where the salt of the earth is going to get its savor if it ever loses it. We're supposed to be the light shining on the mountain top, and most of the time we feel that if the fuse isn't blown at least the circuits are pretty weak. In the final analysis, the issue is whether we really believe the sermons we preach, whether we really believe that Christ is risen from the dead, whether we really believe that the Christian faith is good news, whether we really believe sin, death, error, misery, suffering are eventually to be conquered and eliminated from the human condition. If we do, then we must display enthusiasm no matter how tired or weary or discouraged we feel. If we do not, then we might just as well pack up our things and head for the hills because we are not fit to be priests.

There's a good deal of enthusiasm for prophecy in some clerical circles these days, the Old Testament style of prophecy. To hear some clergy, particularly younger ones describe the matter, the priest in the role of the prophet is to sit in judgment, to come in out of the wilderness and denounce the sinful city. Then he sits back and waits for the Assyrians or hellfire and brimstone to execute the Lord's judgment on the people whom he has already judged. This kind of prophecy is great fun and releases a lot of aggressions. We can assure ourselves of our own virtue and righteousness and we can blame people for failures that otherwise might be credited to our account. Best of all, we don't have to do anything; we don't have to plan; we don't have to organize; we don't have to discuss; we don't have to study; we don't have to learn. All we have to do is denounce.

If our prophetic model is an Amos or Jeremiah, then we are in business. Some of the other Old Testament prophets like Osee might be a little hard to cope with.

However, the point ought to be that ours is not an Old Testament ministry, and that the Prophet par excellence of the New Testament rarely denounced. On the contrary, most of the time his prophetic message was much more akin to that of Osee or Isaiah. The Lord denounced on occasion, and when he did, it was with a vigor that mankind has seldom matched; but most of the time his prophecy was gentle. The Lord's prophetic style specifically was that of a teacher, patiently and carefully but enthusiastically shaping the minds and the hearts of his followers who, by the way, he called his friends. He chided them when they were wrong; he encouraged them when they were weary; he restrained them when they were militant; he praised them when they did well. Above all, he loved them and communicated to them some sense of the passionate enthusiasm which had brought him on his mission.

Therefore, if the priest of the New Testament is a prophet, he is not a man who denounces or destroys. He sees a vision of a better relationship between God and man, and better relationships among men. Then he labors enthusiastically to make these visions a reality. He is a prophet of creation and recreation, not of destruction.

The problem with the Christian message is not that it is a difficult one, despite the efforts of some modern theologians to make it so, but that it is much too good to be true. We would dearly like to believe in life more abundantly, but we are much too cynical to think it possible. The enthusiastic priest is the man who by his life stands as a witness against cynicism. When a priest becomes a cynic, as many, many priests do, then he gives the lie to everything his ministry is supposed to stand for.

Teenagers manifest almost in caricature what all men look for in their religious leaders, a vision of their own dignity, of their value and of the possibilities of life. To men and women who have come to believe that they are worth very little, the priest must, by his love and concern, convey to them that he is enthusiastic about them even if they are not. And to those who have despaired of the possibilities of hope and happiness in their life, the priest must respond by being enthusiastic about their possibilities even if they are not. As I said before, the priest must say to them in the words of the psychologist, Nevitt Sanford, "We are never too old to grow."

A prophet cannot prophesy that which he does not see. If a priest sees little value or worth in himself and little possibility in his own life, then he surely has nothing to communicate to his people. We must be enthusiastic for our people, but we cannot unless we are enthusiastic about ourselves. How strange and almost blasphemous that sounds! The older generation of seminarians were taught to constantly affirm their own worthlessness. The younger generation has absorbed from the cultural milieu an existentialist *angst* which demands that one feel alienated and devoid of enthusiasm. Either of these poses may be adequate to cope with our own self-destructive emotional needs, but neither has much to do with prophecy or the Christian ministry. Neither *angst* nor self-depreciation is the message of the Gospel. The priest who is not an enthusiastic priest is not much of a priest. He will not be an enthusiast unless he believes in himself. Without enthusiasm, he cannot believe in himself for very long. The source of both enthusiasm and self-belief ultimately is the risen Lord Jesus who loves us. Our enthusiasm is only a continuation and manifestation of his.

[11]
Prudence

There was once a young ecclesiastical administrator who after every interview in his office, wrote himself a lengthy memo on exactly what was said so that he would be able to "protect himself" should any question arise in the future as to what was said. He gave up the practice rather quickly because he has gone on to be one of the best administrators in the American Church, but the mentality behind such a practice is by no means limited to one man. We in the clergy were trained to be "safe" which was described as being "prudent." Such "safe" men were promoted, rewarded, given positions of responsibility. It was said of one apostolic delegate to the United States that the highest praise to be bestowed on a churchman was to say, "he's a 'safe' man." Some of the "safe" men that this gentlemen was responsible for bringing into positions of power turned out to be notoriously incompetent at a time in Church history that other qualities besides safety were requisites for leadership.

Prudence as a virtue of the "safe" man was taken to mean a virtue which inclines us to do nothing, or at least nothing which will run any risk of offending the most cautious of our superiors or our subordinates. The "safe" man not only does not do anything risky; he doesn't even do anything that might cause comment. Ideally, he doesn't do anything at all.

I've often wondered what would have happened to the Church if St. Peter had been a "safe" man and unwilling to take the Church outside the walls of Jerusalem or to accept Gentile converts inside the Church. What if St. Paul were a "safe" man and insisted that all Christians must observe the Judaic laws? What if St. Patrick were a safe man and did not want to run the risk of contaminating the Church by bringing it to Celtic barbarians? What if St. Thomas Aquinas were a "safe" man and had not tried to accomplish a marriage between faith and reason? What if Ignatius or St. Vincent DePaul were "safe" men and therefore didn't try to modify the religious life? One could go on and ask these questions indefinitely. If all the clergy and hierarchy of the Catholic Church had been "safe" men, we would still be a small band of fifteen or twenty members huddled near the southern walls of the city of Jerusalem.

If prudence is a virtue, it is obviously a virtue which inclines us to do something more than nothing. It is a virtue which inclines us to do the right thing at the right time. It indicates that if the proper course of action is one which involves considerable risks, the prudent thing to do is to run the risk. Furthermore, given the fact that the Church can accomplish its mission only by taking risks, it would follow that prudence is a virtue which dictates constant risk taking. Therefore, the prudent man is the gambling man, the man who takes carefully calculated risks almost as easily and as naturally as he breathes the air. The prudent priest is, at least in our day and age, an experimenter. He experiments with new techniques, with new ideas and with new relationships for himself. He does not play it safe in his methodology, his ideas or even his own person. It used to be argued that a priest must be careful about entering deep relationships with his people because, if he does, he may become emotionally involved with them and may risk losing his "vocation." It is surely true that if a priest become intimate with his people, he will become deeply involved emotionally, and such involvement may increase the risk that he will leave the priesthood. On the other hand, the refusal to become emotionally involved with one's people does not make an ineffective ministry probable; it makes it certain. So the real alternatives are not a safe ministry and an unsafe one, but an effective ministry in which the priest runs the risk of the human condition, and an ineffective one in absolute safety which may be close to absolute zero.

We must be willing to take chances and to run risks because this is part of the law of life and the law of growth. If there is no risk, there is no growth. If there is no taking of chances, there is old age long before its proper time. He who is able to take risks when he is young will stay young. He who refuses to take risks is old no matter what his age. The "safe" man is free from all dangers, but he can count on a very dull and often uneventful life.

Prudence then is a virtue which motivates us to be gamblers and risk takers, but it does not lead us to be reckless. The priest who thinks that there is nothing particularly wrong in spending a weekend at a motel—in separate cabins of course—with a lonely divorcee is not a risk taker. He's crazy. The wise gambler is the man who calculates the risks, and his risks never exceed those absolutely required by the situation in which he finds himself. He does not seek adventure for its own sake, much less danger because he enjoys it. He experiments because it is important for him to know what the result of the experiment will be.

There are a number of rules that the prudent priest, the risk-taking priest, should keep in mind. First of all, and perhaps most important of all, he does not take risks with other people's happiness. He does not experiment on people as do the immature seminarians who during their summer vacations engage in intense emotional relationships with young females in order that they may get "experience." The happiness, the humanness, the dignity of the human person is not a suitable object for experimentation. We may experiment *together with* other people, but we don't experiment *on* them. Furthermore, we don't trust our own judgments completely when it comes time to decide whether we're turning people into objects.

Secondly, we are very careful as risk takers in not departing from the norms of sound doctrine, intelligent history or functional behavioral sciences. Since we are discreet gambling men, we are well aware of the importance of sound instincts and good taste. When men of taste and sensibility are affronted by an experiment, that ought to be a pretty good sign to us that the risk taking involved is excessive.

Finally, the discreet gambler is a collegial gambler. He does not engage in unilateral action motivated only by his own instincts. He is capable of seeking advice and suggestions from others and of accepting the advice and suggestions when they are offered. He doesn't necessarily give up his own position simply because it is criticized, but neither does he refuse to ponder the possiblility that he might be deceiving himself.

These three rules are merely another way of saying that the discreet gambler is careful to make sure that there are reality checks which enable him to determine whether his risk taking is well calculated or not. The gambler has confidence in himself, or he would not take risks; but he also has quite enough skepticism about himself to realize that unilateral risk taking is a sign not of a confident man, but of the man who is bent on his own self-destruction.

So, our risks must be well calculated, but they also must be taken. The problem with risk taking in the priesthood is not that there are too many risk takers, but that there are not nearly enough. The calculation we have, but the risks we do not have. We do not with John Kennedy say, "why not?" As the legendary pastors of old, we say, "why?" Then we add that we never did it that way before, or that we've always done it this way.

The British General Percival who presided over the incredible military debacle at Singapore was a positive genius for thinking of reasons for not taking action. All the suggestions that were made to him for the defense of Singapore were rejected on one ground or another. So he did nothing to prepare for the Japanese. Even when it was suggested to him that since the Japanese were coming down the Peninsula it might be wise to fortify the undefended part of Singapore which faced the peninsula, he responded that this would be a serious mistake because it would be bad for the morale of the troops. What it did for their morale when the Japanese landed on this undefended part of the island was apparently a question that did not occur to the General. Men of General Percival's personality abound in the Catholic priesthood.

This abundance is somewhat puzzling, at least in the United States, since the ordinary middle class American professional man, at least since 1940, has been well aware that he cannot be successful in his profession without being willing to run risks. The fear of taking chances has been bred in us from our seminary days on. We are afraid of making mistakes; we are afraid of failing; we are afraid of criticisms; we are afraid of the unknown. There is probably no profession in the United States more ready to tremble when someone asks, "What will others say?" than the priesthood. Criticism, even from a handful of people, is usually more than enough to discourage most priests. The mere whisper of a rumor that some priests are saying critical things is enough to cause many of us to quiver. The priesthood, as a reference group is, or at least was until recently, a closely knit and closed-end community of men. We knew all too well that our reputations could be demolished quickly. So what other priests thought and said of us exercised real power on our lives.

The younger generation of clergy is perhaps less concerned about what the Wednesday night bridge club or the Thursday afternoon golf foursome may say about them. But some of these men have merely set up one reference group as a substitute for another. The all-powerful priestly cliques may be dying off with the rest of clerical culture, but the death agony is a long one.

I am afraid that there is something in our training and experiences as priests which leads us to be cowards. Even the most militant among us would dearly like to have the approval of our brothers. The leaders of many of the priest associations in the country who are afraid to lead and would like to have policy made for them by public opinion polls merely reflect on the left side of the spectrum the cowardice that permeates the profession.

One cannot escape, if one is honest, the hard fact that for the priest prudence and fortitude are virtually the same. We cannot ask others to take risks with their lives if we are not willing to stick our heads above the trench. Yet, so many of us seem to be determined to be known as "safe" men, men who never made a mistake because they never did anything at all.

The American priest is great at concealing himself behind the confessional screen, hiding behind his Roman collar, hiding behind the confines of clerical culture, hiding behind the frosty glass of the rectory office, or hiding on picket lines, or in wild, radical coffee house discussions. He was trained to be a coward; he knows how to be very good at cowardice. He was not trained for bravery, but he lives in a time when he has no choice but to be brave. He is told that he must take risks, and all too often he becomes a kamikaze radical bent on his own self-destruction. He probably needs a good course in political sicence, not taught by a puritan with a Ph.D., but by the local precinct captain.

[12]

Prayerfulness

One of the most lively topics in priestly discussion presently is the Breviary. Older clergy marvel at how the younger clergy seem to ignore completely the obligation of the Divine Office; middle aged clergy compare themselves with one another on how far they have progressed from the Breviary obligation as they understood it in the seminary; and younger clergy pride themselves on how many months or even years they can go without even picking up, or even owning a copy of the Roman Breviary. Perhaps the Breviary deserves this fate. It was an inept and outmoded form of prayer. When imposed as it was—and technically still is—under "pain of mortal sin," it readily became a horror for most priests, and one of the first things to be shed when the priesthood began to break loose from the glaciers in which it had been frozen for many years. Presumably, however, no one would be willing to assert that daily readings from the Scripture and the traditions of the Church are positively harmful. We may even live to see the day when a new generation of clergy will insist that it is absolutely necessary that they read something like the Roman Breviary almost every day, if not daily.

We are told in these turbulent times of ours that a young priest need not pray because going to a concert, art exhibition, or even a political protest meeting means more to him than prayer. Or we are told that he need not meditate because group discussion is a greater stimulus to his spiritual growth than meditation. Now, I would not want to be numbered among the opponents of concerts, art exhibitions, protest meetings, or even group discussions. I think all of these events can be very helpful for the human growth of any man's personality and particularly of the priest's personality. But, I don't think that these events are a substitute for prayer. I make this assertion not as a defender of traditional religious values, but as a dispassionate sociologist observing human behavior.

One gets the impression that some of our secularists or radical theologians are just a bit miffed at the Deity because he did not turn out to be what they thought he would be in their parochial school or Sunday school classrooms. Now they are quite proud of themselves when they announce that they no longer pray because any God that they know of couldn't possibly need their prayers.

Surely they do not expect all of us to take this seriously as a great new theological discovery. Even the highly anthropomorphic Yahweh of the Old Testament assured his people that when the chips were down he really couldn't care less for their sacrifices and burnt offerings. Any God that really needs human prayer because it somehow or other enhances his glory is not a God that the authentic Judeo-Christian tradition would consider worth worshipping. Man prays not because God needs the prayer, but because man does. Despite the solemn proclamations of the radical theologian that God is dead, there really is little or no evidence in the behavioral sciences that man's need to pray is any less than in the past, or that he prays any less than he has done in the past. The serious sociologists of religion as opposed to the theological proponents of pop sociology have little or no doubts about man's need for the sacred; nor do they have much question that the sacred is going to persist into the foreseeable future. Unlike the theologians, the sociologists see no reason why secularity and sacredness cannot coexist. On the contrary, they can readily provide all sorts of data from modern and primitive cultures to show that far from being mutually exclusive modalities of human behavior, the sacred and the secular seem to be complementary to one another. Repress the sacred and it will show up in some other fashion, be it the hippies with their beads, drug addicts with their psychedelic trips, far-out rock and roll music, or even a renewed interest in witchcraft. God may be dead, but curiously enough he seems to be undergoing a renaissance.

Prayer then, be it private prayer of a single man, or the public prayer of a community, is, from a sociological viewpoint, a modality of human behavior that is well-nigh universal. Man prays because he has to, because he has a profound need to proclaim his "at oneness" with himself, his fellowman and the strange primal forces which move the universe. No matter how sophisticated he becomes in understanding the mysteries of his own person, the human community or the political world, there still seems to be much more existing beyond the boundaries of his knowledge than there is within those boundaries. There was a time when the physical scientists were persuaded that they had approached the last frontier of the understanding of the physical world. Now they know far better. God, as one physicist has said, is a brilliant mathematician, but also a very tricky one. I am not trying to argue for the existence of God from the fact that many mysteries of the physical universe are unsolved. I am arguing that man's scientific knowledge has not eliminated the mysterious from his life. It is doubtful whether, even if the behavioral and the physical scientists could understand all phenomena within their purview, the ultimate mystery of "why" would be any less mysterious than it is now. From the sociological viewpoint, prayer is man's answer to the mysterious why, the why of the physical world, the why of human society and community and the why of that most mysterious being of all, himself.

I've often been told that there are many men in the world who claim they have no need of prayer and who do not pray. I'm not exactly sure what this argumentation proves. I could respond that there are far more men who do need prayer and who do pray. I could also respond that the men who assert that they do not need prayer might be far happier and far more human if they were able to pray. I could also argue that many wise and learned men do pray, and that the agnostic intellectual who asserts that he does not pray may be a transitional creature. He may be as my teacher, Everett Hughes, once remarked, ". . . a dessicated, dehumanized version of man."

From the sociological viewpoint, therefore, it seems that man does not need to pray only if he can succeed in resolving the mysteries of himself in the human community and the physical universe. Whether it is healthy or even possible to do this would represent a value decision beyond the domain of the social sciences. However, the sociologist is also compelled to note that the man who does not pray does not seem any happier for his independence from the forces of mystery.

But the committed Christian believing in the good news of the Lord Jesus, believing in the Resurrection, believing in the promise of the return, has no desire to cut himself off from liturgical unity with the world and with the human community in which he is immersed. He prays because he knows that through his prayer he seems somewhat more at peace in his relationship with the world, with men, with himself and with God. He knows that peace flows from an increased understanding of the unities in which he is immersed and also from an increased emotional involvement in these unities. He prays publicly because public prayer is a celebration of unity, and he reflects privately because he knows that in these private reflections he comes to understand profoundly the impact of these unities on his life.

In many of the spiritual conferences in the seminary we were persuaded that prayer was a means for going apart from the human condition, for cutting ourselves off from our fellowmen and from the world and for communing alone with God. If this is all prayer is, the youthful radicals would be quite correct in rejecting it. But prayer, even private prayer, even the highest forms of private contemplation, are not and cannot separate man from the unities in which he is immersed. We are rooted in the human condition; we are rooted in the soil of the earth, in the atmosphere we breathe, in the life forces which surge through us. No matter how ecstatic our contemplation, we are still worshipping with a mind that is inescapably linked with the human body, and with a body which is forever a part of the physical cosmos. When the contemplation is over, we return to the human community from which comes the raw material for ecstatic contemplation. Prayer cannot separate man from the human condition nor was it designed to. On the contrary, its main purpose by its very nature is to help man understand the human condition better and be more effectively immersed in it.

For this reason, if the priest is to be the man to whom others turn, the man who is a relational man par excellence, the man whose life and ministry symbolizes unity among the Christian people, he must be a praying man. He clearly presides over the praying community in the liturgy when the Christian community gives thanks to God. A liturgy which does not represent in stylized and exaggerated form a reality that exists in everyday life runs the risk of being, if not a hypocritical liturgy, at least an inadequate one. All Christians, of course, must pray and must joyously celebrate the unities which they share with all men, especially the unities which the Resurrection brings to them. The priest who presides over the praying community must, it seems to me, be especially aware of these unities, and be especially adept in celebrating them, not only around the eucharistic table, but in his daily life.

It is not my intention to use an argument rooted in sociology and psychology to come through the back door to the traditional exercises of piety. Although my argument is rooted in the social sciences, I do not think it is a new argument. The psychology and sociology of prayer described in this book are, in my judgment, not very far removed from prayer as it is described in the Scriptures. Nor do I wish to either restore or destroy traditional piety. In the form in which it was served up to us in our seminary days it was stagnant and moribund, but even in that sorry state it represented a dry academic form of something that was once vital and alive. The insights of the behavioral sciences should not be used to destroy traditional piety, but to renew it and develop it. I will not attempt to defend or attack the Breviary, the rosary, daily Mass, weekly Confession or any specific form of what we used to call "mental prayer." Nor would I be inclined to either attack or defend notebooks of faults in which we kept an accurate record of how many times we succumbed to our dominant vice. It seems to me that such individual practices are largely irrelevant. At one time they helped some human beings. Today they may still help some. But all of these spiritual practices were acts of individual behavior deduced from a tradition, but they were not always explained or defended in keeping with the best insights of the tradition. How that tradition is to be developed and applied in the modern world is a question which I, for one, do not yet feel capable of answering.

Exactly how one meditates on and proclaims the unities is not nearly so important as whether one does so. Furthermore, the personal prayer life of the priest whose role it is to teach others the meaning of the unities is not nearly so important as the fact that by word and example he lives these unities. No one can live that which he does not celebrate and contemplate.

We were told in our seminary days that if we did not pray we would not be good priests. The advice was right, but perhaps for the wrong reason. In the seminary prayer took on an almost superstitious value, a kind of magic relationship established with God that guaranteed that we would not leave the priesthood, would not become an alcoholic or a womanizer. A much more convincing case could be made for prayer on far more humanistic grounds: the man who does not pray is the man who is cut off. The priest who is cut off cannot be a relational man for his people; he cannot be a man to whom others turn because the assertion of the unities of prayer has been inhibited. Liturgy and contemplation keep us in the human condition. There are other ways of remaining in the human condition, but prayer is one of the best. When one's insertion in the human condition involves a commitment to a belief in the Resurrection, there is no alternative to prayer. One cannot be a good priest without prayer because when one does not pray he is cut off from the Resurrection.

Therefore, when we priests do not pray we are increasing our level of alienation. To the extent that we are alienated we are ineffective as leaders and relational men. Priests who proclaim with some degree of secret or overt pride that they have not prayed in a long time are proclaiming that their priesthood is diminishing. The priest who knows in his heart that he has stopped praying is a priest whose priesthood is in danger, not because he has lost a superstitious charm, but because he is cutting himself off. Prayer isn't going to solve all of mankind's problems; but without prayer, we cannot even begin to solve them.

Epilogue

It is difficult to be optimistic about the present condition of the priesthood—not impossible—but difficult. The old world, as we said in the beginning, is in a state of collapse. New structures are slow to emerge. Many are hesitant and uncertain about their own futures. What will the Church and the world be like at the end of the 1970's? Will there be room for us in either? If we do not get out now, is there not a strong possibility that both world and Church will leave us behind? So much has already collapsed, will not everything collapse?

In this book, and in much of my other writings, I have tried to argue that ours is a crisis of opportunity, and not of deterioration; that it is far more important that something new is being born than that something old is dying. Yet one sees the death all around and must look very hard to find a new birth. The priesthood no longer enjoys the respect that it once had; young men are not flocking to it as they did even a decade ago; and the steady stream of lonely, bitter, angry, disillusioned men continues to flow out of the ranks of the priesthood. Some of them tell us that they are happy, that they are finding fulfillment in the real world, that their work is relevant, that they have at last come to the real world and are able to be men. They argue that, if we had courage and integrity, we would leave ourselves. The only reason we stay, we are told, is because we need the money and are afraid to risk ourselves in the marketplace of career occupation.

A good deal of this can be discounted. How many of those who leave the priesthood find the world outside any better than the world in the priesthood is problematic. For some of them their departure from the priesthood is, indeed, part of the process of growing up, of maturing emotionally. But for most of them one fears that there is little maturation involved. They move from one context of unhappiness to another context of unhappiness, and their claims of relevance or moral superiority or of validated manhood are simply pathetic attempts at self-justification. That men should leave the priesthood if they are unhappy in it is, undoubtedly, an improvement, both for them and for the priesthood. It does not follow, however, that the priesthood caused their problems, or that departure from the priesthood will solve any such problems. The priest who permits himself to be discouraged—at least for lengthy periods of time—by the departure of others from the ministry is permitting his own integrity and his own commitment to be evaluated by other people's actions and not by his own standards. Those who leave the priesthood because of contagion or fear that the ship is sinking must be judged to be men who lack both strength and personal integrity. They may also lack faith.

To say that someone lacks faith is not to say that he does not believe in the infallibility of the Pope, or the Virgin birth, or the existence of angels. It is to say, rather, that he has no core of personal convictions around which his life is organized. This may well, indeed, be the root of most of the other problems in the priesthood: the way we were recruited, the way we were trained, the kinds of work situations in which we were placed—none of these helped us to develop strong internal convictions. Our faith, such as it was, was propped up and sustained by external structures. The charming old Italian gentleman who opened his window permitted a lot of those structures to be knocked over, and now we must survive on those personal commitments and convictions that are at the core of our personality. Some of us are shocked to find that there isn't much in the core.

If I were asked what the most serious problem facing the priesthood today is, I would be forced to answer that it is precisely the lack of serious, internalized convictions. The absence of convictions manifests itself, I think, in two ways: superficiality and immaturity. Theologians are saying that the priest is essentially a liturgist, a man who presides over the eucharistic liturgy and is in no other way different from the rest of the Christian people. As one young priest put it to me: "Why should I visit the sick any more than any other member of the Christian community?" Another one observed: "Why should I attempt to exercise leadership charisma in the Christian community? Is it not possible that many other members of the community have more of that charisma than I do?"

Now I will concede that I am not a theologian (though some of my best friends are theologians, and if questioned whether I would want my sister to marry a theologian, I would answer that my sister *is* a theologian). But I have tried, through the years since the end of the Council, to keep in touch with the best of the theological writing on the priesthood, particularly as it has been done by men like Karl Rahner, Edward Schillebeeckx, Hans Kung and Walter Kasper. I should like to make a number of observations about the writings of these men:

1] If there is one position that they universally reject, it is the notion that the priest is primarily a liturgist. Those American clergymen who persist in thinking of the priest as one who leads the liturgy and one who in other respects is no different than anyone else are repeating a theology that is at least five years out of date.

2] The European theologians also are unanimous in arguing that the priest's principal function is that of leadership of the Christian community. In Walter Kasper's words.

> Finally, the Church becomes a reality in the communal and reciprocal ministry of love. Here, too, the priestly office is empowered to further the unity of the community by its overall direction. This direction is not to be embodied in authoritarian decrees and measures of brute force. On the contrary, it is meant to bring the various charisms into meaningful and fruitful contact with one another. It is meant to discover and awaken these charisms, to foster them and give them room to operate, while at the same time keeping them in their proper place and admonishing them when they endanger Church unity.

Kasper goes on to say:

> The Eucharist, insofar as it is the sign and symbol of

Church unity, simply cannot be separated from the unity of the Church. Neither, then, can the power to celebrate the Eucharist be separated from the power to lead the Church. The authoritative sacramental ministry of the priest can only be appreciated correctly if it is integrated once again with his ministry on behalf of the unity of the Church community.

If we try to understand the priestly ministry in terms of the function of community leadership and the duty of promoting Church unity, then we can also accord him a role in present-day society. For the unity of the Church is not closed in upon itself; it stands as a sign and a sacrament of the unity of the world. The priestly ministry, then, involves a broader ministry on behalf of the peace and unity of mankind. It is closely tied up with one of the deepest and most pervasive longings of contemporary mankind.*

In other words, those young clergy who argue that they should not be expected to lead, or that it makes no difference whether they visit the sick simply do not understand contemporary theology.

3] The priest is seen not merely as the one who unites the members of the Christian community, one with another, but as one who takes the lead in being the sacrament (that is to say, the efficacious symbol) of the unity between the Church and the world. In other words, there is a vast variety of ways in which the priest exercises his unifying role, and any attempt to limit that to one particular form of ministry, one particular kind of work, or even to argue that one sort of ministry is superior to other ministries, is

* *Concilium*, Vol. 3, No. 5 (March, 1969), pp. 15-18.

theologically and historically—as well as sociologically—
in error.

4] The priestly role is a charismatic one; there is bound
to be some tension between the "office" of the priest and
the "charism" of the priest. On this subject this long quote
from Kasper seems to come to the core of the problem:

> The priestly ministry, then, is never simply a job or
> one's "life work." Here faith in Jesus becomes something
> more than the general foundation for one's life as a
> human being; it becomes the distinctive foundation of
> one's whole professional existence. Bearing witness to
> Christ in his professional life, the priest serves as a symbol
> and a deputy of the community that is entrusted to his
> care. In both what he is and what he does, he is "for
> others." In short, the function of community leadership
> has a thoroughgoing ontological aspect.
>
> The unity of the Church, which the priestly function is
> meant to serve, is not just a sociological reality; it is also,
> and primarily, a theological reality. It is a unity in one
> Lord and one Spirit; hence it can only be served in and
> through the Holy Spirit. The ministry of community
> leadership involves a real theological charism as well as
> a human charism. The priestly office cannot be carried
> out by purely sociological functions. On the other hand,
> we cannot view this charism as something basically
> inimical to institutional and official structures. There can
> be no essential split between charism and office.
>
> There is, however, a continuing tension between office
> and charism, and it is rooted in the interim nature of
> the Church. Because the Church is "on the way" from
> the old to the new era, the unity of office and charism
> is not something "given"; it persists as a duty to be

accomplished, and the difference between the two realities is a fact that is experienced by every priest.*

5] Gerald Broccolo, in a recent contribution to *Concilium*, suggests in passing that a man should be chosen for the priesthood precisely because he does display those charismatic qualities which mark him as "inspirited." The priestly charisma, then, both human and theological, is such that the priest is both born to lead and ordained to lead. The priest is the man in whom the Spirit dwells in a very special way.

This brings us to the second manifestation of lack of conviction in the priesthood, for if one freely chooses to be superficial, if one freely chooses to live in a context where critical questions are not only unanswered, but treated as unanswerable, then one can legitimately be accused of immaturity. To break out of superficiality—to seek integrating answers to difficult questions— is the mark of the mature, well-organized personality, the personality which has enough convictions to be able to seek clarification of convictions when such clarification is required. The priest who really doesn't seem to want to answer the question— What is a priest?—is one who is deliberately choosing to keep his own convictions truncated, and he is doing so because he is afraid to run the risk of moving beyond superficiality toward understanding and wisdom. What he is saying is that "things are bad enough now. If I run the risk of learning more, then I might make it impossible for me to get out. I will remain superficial. I will persist in truncating my convictions precisely at a time when I have the option of getting out should the tension become

* *Ibid.*

too severe." There is an element of the self-fulfilling prophecy about all this, of course, but that in its own way is just another manifestation of immaturity. The ultimate in immaturity, it seems to me, is the man who leaves the priesthood simply because it is now possible to leave—possible, that is, in the sense that the social and cultural inhibitions against leaving have been substantially weakened. As long as departing from the priesthood was not a serious option, this man would not have left. But once it becomes a serious option, he *must* leave, for it is intolerable to him that any serious option be available and remain unexercised. He has neither the convictions nor the personality strength to resist his own impulses. An option is there, and it simply has to be exercised because it sets up dynamic demands simply by its availability—a dynamic which he is too weak to resist.

There are many of us in the priesthood, then, who were recruited and trained for a priestly ministry that no longer exists, and we lack the depth, the commitment, the conviction, the integrity, and the strength to survive in the present confusion and uncertainties. Presumably those who are being trained in the new seminary systems will be more mature and sophisticated, with greater self-awareness and greater personal depth. Presumably they will be able to handle the crisis which is too much for us. Yet it would be foolish to resign ourselves to being the last of the old breed, especially when, in the context of the present essay, the old breed includes almost everybody over twenty-eight. If we lack conviction, which is to say if we lack faith, that does not mean that we cannot acquire conviction. If we are immature, it does not mean that we cannot grow. If we have been unable to cope with the present confusion and uncertainty, it does not mean that we are unable to learn how to cope with it.

If we leave behind theoretical discussion of the problems facing the priesthood and take a good, hard, careful look at the priestly ministry the way it is being exercised at present, we must conclude that the astonishing thing is not the lack of conviction and commitment, but the astonishing commitment and conviction which exists among so many priests. It is not surprising that some priests have lacked the flexibility and maturity necessary to cope with the change in the church. What is surprising is that so many have demonstrated astonishing flexibility and maturity. What is puzzling is not that some American priests are leaving the priesthood, but rather that so many of them are staying. Given the kinds of backgrounds from which we come and the kinds of training we have received, it is well-nigh incredible that we have done as well as we have. Maybe the biggest problem of all is that we don't have enough self-esteem or self-confidence to recognize how well we have done under extremely trying circumstances.

What an astonishing irony it would be if maybe, just maybe, future generations look back on the priesthood of the 1960's and the 1970's and, along with Winston Churchill's future generations of Englishmen, mutter something about "their finest hour."

And then it will turn out that a lot of people have missed the boat—a boat which is Peter's bark moving briskly over the waves as the strong winds of the Spirit blow it whither He will.